# Pimpnosis

# Pimpnosis

Tracy Funches and Rob Marriott

HarperEntertainment
*An Imprint of* HarperCollins*Publishers*

HarperCollins books may be purchased for educational, business, or sales promotional use. For information please write: Special Markets Department, HarperCollins Publishers Inc., 10 East 53rd Street, New York, NY 10022.

FIRST EDITION

*Designed by Jo Obarowski*

Printed on acid-free paper

Library of Congress Cataloging-in-Publication Data

Funches, Tracy.

Pimpnosis/by Tracy Funches & Rob Marriott.—1st ed.

p.  cm.

ISBN 0-06-621165-4 (hc: acid-free paper)

1. Pimps—United States.  2. Pimps—United States—Pictorial works.  I. Marriott, Rob.  II. Title.

HQ144 .F83 2002

.306.74'0973—dc21              2002024033

02  03  04  05  06  TP  10  9  8  7  6  5  4  3  2  1

*Dedicated to the game*

# Contents

# Message from the
# Old School

If you were to delve into the heart of hip-hop culture and ask a dozen young urban hipsters what a pimp or a player is, you'd get at least a dozen different answers. The consensus, though, would be that a player/pimp is not much more than a modern-dress Casanova.

In my day, that kind of ladies' man simply would have been labeled a "playboy" and certainly never mentioned in the same breath as an accomplished hustler. Nowadays there are legions of young black hustlers and pretenders out there who identify themselves as players and pimps. Most of them don't have the foggiest idea about the psychology of the game they imagine themselves to be playing. Most of the rap stars, hip-hop singers, thugs, gang-bangers, and others who *call* themselves players are completely unconscious of the fact that nothing could be further from the truth. No intelligent player from the past ever needed a gun or a crew of thugs or worked a menial job to survive.

So who am I? And what are my credentials to speak with authority on such an unauthorized subject? I'm a bona fide true player from a bygone era, now affectionately called the Old S'cool. I was there when the contemporary hustler was renamed, and believe me when I say that its original intent shared nothing with today's misrepresentation of it. In the early sixties we were the first generation of young black hustlers from the urban underworld centers of America to call ourselves "players." It was a term of endearment and respect applied *only* to those of the criminal element, the secret underworld of black hustlers, who managed to achieve, against all odds, a high level of illegal material success from their hustling abilities and wit alone.

♦ ♠ ♥ ♣

The book you're about to dive into constitutes one of the rare occasions when our particular lifestyle as hustlers and survivors is fairly portrayed, without ever yielding to stereotype or comedic misrepresentation. Seeing these pictures and reading this story, you will discover that Once upon a Time in the Ghetto, long before the emergence of ballers, shot callers, high rollers, new jacks, and the like, we were the first of the easy-money boys. We were the slicksters and tricksters and gamesters who coined the ultimate title of honor and respect—player!—and bestowed that honorific epithet upon those who deserved it.

Black folklore is replete with stories of the suave, sophisticated, and superstylish black hustler, yet his underworld tales are all but ignored by the popular culture that tends to favor and romanticize the gangster exploits of foreign groups over those who were homegrown. This is one of our stories. It is rooted in the rich subcultural history that we hustlers descend from. Sociologists the world over have queried themselves silly trying to figure out how it is that we, the criminal element of the socially disadvantaged, have managed to survive, here in this bottomless pit of racial disparity and social despair. These pages will be your guide to questions those sociologists couldn't answer, and ones you never even thought to ask. So before we older players from an age gone by follow jazz, disco, and soul music into a mist of vague remembrances, this story will shed light on the history of an infamous lifestyle. It will serve as a testament to the reality of a world that has been greatly misunderstood and grossly maligned, but never truly entered by those who stood outside it—until now.

*Chicago Michael Ace*

# Pimpnosis

# *Introduction*

The curtains part, the lights dim, and the screen goes from black to night: we are in the city, no moon. Rain-slick streets but the storm is over, a cloudless night serves as backdrop to the hyperbright streetlights. Niggahs is in the background talking shit, drowned out by the hissing sound of fat tires pealing on wet blacktop. It's a customized Fleetwood Coupe Sedan Landau Brougham Eldorado deVille, a Cadillac on steroids. Gangster whitewalls, TV antenna in the back, sunroof top, white leather seats, tinted windows, and a metal-flake magenta body that seems to drag out for about half a block before it pulls to a stop and cuts off the talk in midsyllable. The music starts, the bass kicks in. The back door opens, and the camera cuts to a leg stepping out—hand-tailored polyester double-knit white bell bottom; translucent dress sock, the kind requiring a garter; gleaming white shoe on a two-inch platform, three-inch heel. The gui-

tars start playing, and as we settle into our seats and grab the popcorn, we know exactly where we're at and who we're dealing with.

Or so we think.

♦　♠　♥　♣

Pimps. Players. Macks.

Few subjects get reactions more extreme. For every young wanna-be who smiles at the fantasy of his own harem—hot and cold running women at his beck and call— there are a thousand people who shake their heads in righteous indignation at the mere mention of the word. Pimps are despised, demonized, shrouded in stereotype, and cut in caricature. Yet for all the moral disgust and disdain they evoke in all of us—even in other hustlers and criminals—we are still fascinated by them and the world they live in.

Pimping is everywhere these days. Their modern rites, lingo, and sense of excess still influence everything from fashion to music, commerce, language, and sex.

Youth culture wordwide is obsessed with pimps. Songs like Jay-Z's "Big Pimpin'" spend weeks at the top of the Billboard charts, and the films and soundtracks from the so-called blaxploitation era of the seventies enjoy enduring popularity. Hip-hop and rock luminaries like Snoop Dogg and Kid Rock go out of their way to emulate the pimp image. Daytime talk shows can't get enough of them. Websites devoted to the subject garner millions of hits a month, and documentaries like HBO's *Pimps Up, Ho's Down* have even made celebrities out of former pimps like Bishop Don Juan and Pimpin' Kenny Ivey. It's undeniable: pimps have a mystique about them that refuses to go away. Perhaps it's because pimping taps into something older than we can possibly imagine.

The practice itself is thousands of years old—it can be seen in ancient Greece, Renaissance Italy, early modern Japan, and the Bible. If prostitution is the oldest profession, then pimping can't be that far behind.

But in the cultural imagination, pimping is 100 percent American. Forget the temple prostitutes of ancient Israel, the courtesans of France, or even the *zegen*—legalized pimps who were openly part of Edo, Japan. To many people around the world, the black American version is the ultimate definition of the flesh peddler. Former slaves recreated the age-old profession in their own image: the rhythmic limping, the flashy jewelry, the exaggerated clothes, and the outrageous accoutrements are all peculiar to the black imagination. In so doing, the American mack captured the wide-eyed imagination of the entire world.

The image of the pimp is so deeply ingrained in the national subconscious that it is now full-blown Americana. We see pimp influence reflected in everything from Elvis's outrageous jumpsuits to current popular slang. But the movies and media have shaped our vision of the pimp with a cartoon of the black hustler that has little to do with the reality of pimping. For one, the cartoon hustler presents all pimps as the same—loathsome, ignorant, and above all clownish.

In reality there are all kinds of pimps and many more variations of hustler. Macks are distinct from players and players distinct from pimps. To understand this shifting hierarchy of vice, one must truly be of this underworld. In fact, it is the contention of many full-blooded pimps that "too many lames attempt to claim the name and the fame but ain't got the game." A pimp, according to most, is a man who deals strictly in hos. Pussy is his sole hustle. Any sidetracking disqualifies one from the title of certified pimp. A mack, on the other hand, is someone who has the ability to "game" both legally and illegally. A player qualifies as anyone with even a modicum of hustle skills. But even among pimps there are categories and subcategories—gorilla pimps, finesse pimps, sneaker pimps, and king pimps to name just a few. Self-proclaimed high-class pimp Alfred "Bilbo" Gholson suggests there are fifty-two varieties in all and at least as many different approaches to the game. Simply put, pimps in this country come from all walks of life, both sexes, and all races and classes. Some are highly individualistic style messiahs, while others are master criminals raised in a centuries-old tradition of violence and misogyny. These are the street-corner Machiavellis who've learned all the deviant ways of what Bilbo calls "the sweet science of sin." All aiming to realize the real American dream: to live a life of wealth, power, and sex by working as little as humanly possible.

Most pimps believe they were "born pimpin'"—claiming the life was their calling and they are simply doing what comes natural. But pimping is far from natural. Trafficking in flesh requires a complex of skills not easily cultivated and information not easily acquired. To truly pimp one must be a jack-of-all-trades with some command of accounting, psychology, and poetry. In other words, one must be a confidence man par excellence. One also must have a sense of timing and an eye for detail and be a master of the intangible techniques of persuasion and self-promotion. Even beyond that, pimping demands that you maintain a desolate heart, an interior cold and cruel enough to "let a ho be a ho" no matter what the cost. One must choose money over love, money over sex, money over all that is holy. Emotions, soft feelings, have no place in such a cutthroat game.

To be a pimp is also to accept suffering as part of the price of vice. Not only the suffering of your women as they wear their bodies out in the streets and motel rooms but also your own. Veteran pimps talk about their stripes—the painful, sometimes near-death experience that comes with the pimp's chintz glamour. Police brutality, the ceaseless wandering, the knife and gun fights, the deaths of friends, family, and workers are all possibilities that come with the terrain. Everyone is familiar with the stories of children who are forced or fooled into sexual slavery, the women who waste their lives and bodies in service of their man. But the pimp and ho function as a symbiote, and as the ho goes so goes the pimp. In the end, the vast majority of so-called macks and players end up spent,

strung out, and desperate. Even before the glories of the life are gone, the fancy clothes can barely conceal the ravages of corruption. The scars all tell stories of their own.

Before you is the collection of several years of difficult and willful research. To gather these stories, we entangled ourselves in an assortment of underworld personalities who were at times shady, comical, tragic, and dark. Names have been changed to protect the innocent and guilty alike. Some characters are composites of the people we ran across in our travels in order to give ourselves greater freedom to reveal the deeper sides of the game.

Our main character is named Twilight. Through him the text depicts the very real dangers, insecurity, and psychological terrain of the prototypical player. While the story plumbs the depth of myth, lore, and legend, the photographs by Tracy Funches traverse the breadth of pimp actuality.

Never have we had such intimacy with the modern pimp. These rare images bring home the reality of the mack life, cutting the distance between reality and our misplaced perceptions. Funches's camera captures it all: the soft mink on ruddy skins, the candy paint against asphalt streets, the dulled-out eyes and neglected teeth. Tracy captures not just the flash and style but the internal corruption that is the price of vice.

Even with all the images of pimps in popular culture, many admirers of "the life" really don't understand what they are celebrating or emulating. What does it mean to be a pimp? How do you convince a woman to rent out her body and then give you all the money? Why does a ho ho in the first place? And if she does, why the hell would she want to give her hard-earned money to a pimp? These are just some of the questions we attempt to address in this volume.

♦　♠　♥　♣

Modern consumer life is based on one simple fact: sex sells. Sex sells everything. Look at a newsstand and see how many magazines pimp scantily clad women on the covers. Find a liquor ad that doesn't look like it's promoting a porn movie. Watch an hour of music videos and pay attention to how many don't use sex as lure and weapon. Almost everything that's sold uses sex as its selling point. In a society in which sex and commerce are perpetually bound together, pimps are not a weird aberration of our social fabric— they're the logical extension of the status quo.

But it doesn't end with sex. Think about your job. If you're like most, you do work somebody else could do, and you'd let anybody take your place in a heartbeat if you could still collect that check. On paper you're getting paid for what you produce, but deep down inside you know that money is compensation for what you're giving up, what you're not doing, what you're not being. You may not be spreading your legs or walking the streets, but you know you're getting screwed. At least we're getting paid for it, right?

Guess what that makes you.

You're not alone in this pyramid scheme of misery. If you're not in charge, you might get "incentives" to cushion the bleak reality: a bonus, a raise, or shares of the company stock . . . maybe even a promotion to lieutenant. But is that because you're loved, or is that because the company knows damn well how to make it hard for you to leave the crib and the so-called good life? No matter how high up the ladder you are, there's always somebody making a profit on your hard work—and taking the lion's share of the credit and the proceeds.

Guess what that makes them.

This reality is everywhere. Pimps and hos are just the bare-bones, street-level equivalent of common practices that can be found anywhere. Look at banks, music industry contracts, and even credit-card debt. All share in the pimp dynamic.

And this dynamic—the one that makes us pimps and hos at work or in our relationships with our chosen corporations—doesn't just up and disappear when it comes to our personal lives, either. We all know someone who married for money or security instead of love. But is it really that unholy? Love as a basis for marriage is a fairly modern invention. At one time, before women could even own property, it was understood that the bride was the property. In ancient Rome a marriage was sealed when the groom bought the bride from his father-in-law for a penny, and fathers looking for an advantageous match—whether it was about combining kingdoms or gaining acreage—pimped out their daughters to the highest bidders. Even Abraham, father of Christianity, Judaism, and Islam revealed his inner pimp in Genesis 12:10–19.

But pimp as power dynamic is not pimping as lifestyle. This life, the darkest and most extreme example of that dynamic, is now its rarest form. It's the end of pimping as we've known it. No, there's no shortage of men willing to help women sell their bodies and take money for the favor; there's also no shortage of women willing to have sex for money and then give that money to men who act as their agents. These folk who wholly commit themselves to the complex creed and netherworld etiquette of the pimp life are fewer in number. The current spotlight on this world may play to the vanity of some, but for the most hardcore of flesh peddlers such attention is bad for business. The fantabulous hats and shiny cars, the video cameos and movie roles, can serve as targets for indictments in the war against illegal prostitution.

Therefore, the flamboyant pimp is a holdover, a vestige of a bygone era, a time when visibility was less of a liability. More and more pimps work from in the anonymity and safety of the Internet, or the escort ad in the back of the newspaper, where the consumer of a pimp's product never needs to know that the pimp exists. The culture of surveillance has spawned a new brand of pussy hustler, what they call the space-age pimp, a less flamboyant, techno-savvy breed, who chooses to dress his cars in chrome and high-tech paint than dress himself up in gators and pinstrips. What seems like a blossoming in the public mind is really a final flowering. Soon, the American pimp will be off the radar, surfing the lower frequencies, more myth than reality.

The photographs in this book chronicle this soon-to-be-lost world. We believe the examination of the pimp life provides dark revelations about life in a world driven by sex, power, and commerce. Photographer Tracy Funches captures this world up close, giving us a keyhole glimpse of a world few outsiders could ever hope for. Born in Mississippi and schooled at the Chicago Art Institute, for the last fourteen years Tracy has been taking portraits and documenting the shadowy sides of subcultures all over the world: streetscapes in Ensenada, Mexico; extreme youth culture in Tokyo; the hip-hop community in Paris; Players' Balls in the United States. He brings a powerful understanding of light, composition, and above all humanity to the pictures many people don't want to see. Here he has recorded two generations of pimps—the underground gatherings, the old ho strolls, and the various bars, taverns, and strip clubs where the true stomp-down certified pimps ply their craft.

Looking into the eyes of the pimps who populate this book, you might feel a kind of embarrassment for them and for yourself as you confront the unguarded ambition, avarice, lust, grief, and despair. Tracy documents his subjects without judging them, glorifying them, or making them exotic. In return, he captures the vainglorious style, danger, and pose of these outlaws who loom so large in the American imagination. And like the best documentary photography these pictures invite us to confront hardline realities in spite of their beauty. In essence, the pictures and text attempt to wrench the humanity of these elusive and complex folk from under the heavy weight of our preconceived notions. In this pursuit, we've crafted what follows: not a celebration of pimping and not an exposé but a gimlet eye on this mysterious world in all its dark beauty.

# Sold, Not Told

The snow started really coming down and someone chose number 1605 on the jukebox at Marty's Lounge, "Neither One of Us." While Gladys Knight's warm, husky vocals infiltrated the cigarette smoke and barroom chatter, JoJo, proprietor of Marty's, was looking to close up. The crowd from earlier in the evening had dwindled to the degenerate drinkers and a few regulars: Luther, Milk, Sherm, Miss Nicole, and a cop from the precinct who partook of the pleasures of the back room. A few gang-bangers and some of the lap dancers chatted over darts on the far side of the bar. All of them were shadows now, under the rhythmic red and blue lights pulsing along the mirrors, glancing at the early morning showing of *Cool Hand Luke* on the two TVs.

The cop looked down at his watch, peered outside at the falling snow, and said, "Put that last one on the tab, Jo."

"S'all gravy, baby," JoJo responded. The cop said his good-byes to the dancers and then rushed out like he had an appointment.

Two minutes later a champagne-colored Cadillac sidles up to the curb, looking pretty as a newborn in the falling snow. It was Twilight. Everybody from Madison knew his car. He was styling with a pouty little Newport-smoking Cambodian girl getting lost in a sable. He pushed through the front door with a storm cloud over his features, moving at a faster clip than anyone had ever seen him move. Sensing trouble, JoJo and Luther, his unofficial security, raised up.

Something was all kinds of wrong. Twilight? In a Caddy? On a weekday? Weekdays, Twilight usually picked up his girls from the various bars in a dusty Buick. For him to bring out the Cadillac, on a Wednesday, all conspicuous, was completely out of character. So was slamming doors open and coming into a spot, ice grilling, looking like he wanted to eat a man.

He was showing out.

Sherm was too busy getting dead off Jack Daniel's and pop to ever know what hit him. He'd been in a funk since he walked in three hours earlier, throwing 'em back like there was a fire in his gut that only whiskey could put out. He slitted his eyes open just in time to catch the bright sting of Old No. 7 in his face, followed by the flat end of a cell phone smashed into the bridge of his nose, followed by nasty lashes and vicious kicks and stomps that didn't stop until JoJo finally pulled Twilight away from Sherm's fallen body. For a momentary eternity nary a soul moved.

"I'm hearing you out here biting hands that fed you. Takin' niggahs lives away. And then out here having motherfuckin' drinks like shit wasn't gonna get back to us. You fuckin' outta order, niggah." He hissed through gritted teeth with a final kick. "You's a dead man walkin', Jack." Then Twilight spat, turned, and rode out. Sherm rolled around on the floor, blinded and moaning in pain.

People talked about that night for a good long time. Word got around that Sherm had snitched his way out of the joint, but that was too hard to believe. Not Sherm. Sherm was a stand-up cat, not to mention Twilight's cousin, his blood, his brother pimp from childhood. It didn't make sense to anyone. Later, when someone said there was no way Sherm could have been out of stir so fast unless he went and named names, the murmurs got louder. But no one could pin anything on him, and by then it didn't matter, because he wasn't Sherm anymore. He was just this one-eyed drunken ghost on the street who used to be Mack Sherm once upon a time, used to be ace-boon-coon to Twilight. Used to be. And then, one day, he was just gone.

Before that night, Twilight and Sherm were closer than brothers, but it wasn't just what he did to Sherm that rattled people. No one knew Twilight to be violent like that with *anybody*. No one but his girls had ever seen him raise his hand in violence, or even raise his voice above a whisper. Not that he hadn't been young in these streets, riding around with a .38 in an ankle holster, but that was ancient history. He looked down on violence nowadays—guerrilla tactics were beneath him. So however serious he was about what he said to Sherm, and what he did, the performance had to be for effect, for public consumption. And the effect was strong. Folks tripped on how *pimp* the man kept it, even in his most savage moments he moved like liquid, like a movie. Twilight blinded Sherm in one eye, and finished the man as a pimp, but he never even sullied the suit he was wearing while he did it. In the eyes and mouths of the few witnesses that night, Twilight's legend metastasized. Still, fast as it flew from mouth to ear, it wasn't so much news as confirmation of what everybody already thought: for all his cool, his charisma, his easy charm, Twilight walked on the dark side; he was a man to reckon with, not to fuck with. But no matter how much people in the life like to say they were born to it, Twilight wasn't born like this.

It took a lot to bring him here.

# *Pimp by Blood*

Twilight had never asked himself, *What makes a man a pimp?* He just lived the answer. But six weeks before the incident at Marty's, when it was still all good between them, Twilight and Sherm went to the big funeral, and for the first time in his working life, Twilight was starting to question who he was, what he had become, and how, and why. A day that should have been sad yet warm, honoring the passing of his mentor, King Sugar Charmaine, was tainted by the bitter flavor of a bile he couldn't wash away, no matter how much he drank. His mind just kept flashing on the same words: *What's the point?* He wanted to tell the source to just shut the fuck up, but it was no good, because there was no point; the voice was his own.

Charmaine's family, friends, and associates arrived in twos and fours, quickly turn-

ing the service into a big-time hustlers' convention. If you can judge a man by the people who bury him, Charmaine was an S-Class hustler. Boss players came out to see him off. The infamous Frankie Valentine and his wife, Liza, one of the great confidence women to come out of St. Louis, flew in from Phoenix to say their good-byes. Top-flight players like Icy Duck came in from his hideaway in Guam. The McNeals, Michael Spade, and some of Chi-town's premiere mack men made their way back to Chicago's west side to pay their respects. There was Mojo out of D.C. and his partner, Pimp Vogue, along with Old Man Hennessy and Sir Mackey.

A particular well-known point guard for a particular well-known basketball team was there with his brothers, and an internationally renowned pop singer who had his roots in the Chi came to pay their respects. Many others sent gigantic bouquets and their regards—wreaths the size of tractor-trailer tires, seven-foot horseshoes of roses with his name written in rose petals. Among the absent was a Chicago bluesman who apologized for not being there in the flesh. In his place he sent a massive wooden sculpture of the African deity Shango, which stood near the casket and glared at everyone as they viewed the body. The Feds made it too, taking pictures of the guests and their license plates.


Here Lies the Body of

Lonnie "King Sugar" Charmaine Jr.

1958–1999

"My Jesus Mercy"


To call King Sugar simply a pimp would be to whittle his whole life down to a condemnation, but pimping was what he did. He never shied from the title or the life it meant, and if his funeral was any measure, Sugar kept it pimp to the last day. Many of his women and former women, several of whom he had lived with, sat side-by-side in matching white outfits. His oversized casket was decorated with emblems of his prowess in the game. Julianne, his bottom woman and common-law wife for the last thirteen years; his sons, Jason, T.J., and Savior; and the rest of his family sent him to the great beyond in a state of bling. He lay there under the huge explosions of lilies, gardenias, and orchids, his face a little bloated but with a Mona Lisa smirk, wads of hundreds stuffed into the pockets of his white silk suit, platinum fetishes around his neck, diamond tennis bracelets on each wrist, and a bottle of Crystal lying on either side of him. There was a ring on every manicured finger, and his hands rested atop three stacks of hundred-dollar bills fanned out across his stomach. Used to be the man was a mountain of muscle, but rich food and the easy life had sent him out before his time.

But he was going out proper—the casket itself had a Cadillac hood ornament, like he'd be driving himself to the next world in style.

Some laughed and whispered, some sniffled and cried, some didn't say a word, but everyone said they'd fixed him up good, the words floating around the parlor like it was the quote of the day.

Somebody was singing that old hymn, that old workhorse, "The Last Mile of the Way."

> *When I've gone the last mile of the way . . .*
> *I will rest at the close of the day . . .*

It was an old man singing, with a voice like scotch and leather, a gaunt old man in a suit that maybe fit him like a glove back in the day but now hung loose, making him look like an ancient kid in his big brother's Sunday best. Everyone asked who he was and eventually assumed he was a cousin or an uncle.

He just kept on singing.

*And I know there are joys that await me . . .*
*When I've gone the last mile of the way.*

Aside from a laugh here and there, the women talked softly. The men mostly smoked and joked, even if they didn't crank the volume. But Twilight, who'd never really attended church, kept swallowing hard and wishing they'd all shut up and let the man sing. He swallowed hard again and blinked his eyes, and somehow the man was gone and the preacher was wrapping up whatever it was he just said with Psalm 121.

"I will lift up mine eyes unto the hills from whence cometh my help."

"Yes, Lord" from one of the women, followed by laughter and someone's "Shh!"

The preacher went on. "My help cometh from the Lord who made heaven and earth. He will not suffer thy foot to be moved."

"Mmm-hmm."

"That's right!"

"Shh!"

The preacher cleared his throat. "He that keepeth thee will not slumber. Behold, He that keepeth Israel shall never slumber nor sleep."

"I know *I* don't!"

"The Lord is thy keeper. The lord is the shade upon thy right hand."

"C'mon, y'all!"

The preacher picked up the pace. "The sun shall not smite thee by day, nor the moon by night. The Lord shall preserve thee from all evil.

"He shall preserve thy soul. The Lord shall preserve thy going out and thy coming in from this time forth and even forevermore amen."

"A-*men!*"

Twilight tried to keep it together as he and the other straining pallbearers raised up the casket, but all those feelings kept welling up inside him. When they were closing the coffin he caught himself shooting nervous looks at Charmaine's corpse, having crazy thoughts like any second the man would rise up from the dead, pull out a Dunhill, and start draggin' on it. But that wasn't gonna happen. Charmaine's death was the latest in a string of bad turns for Twilight, and the crescendo of a rising doom he'd been feeling for the last couple of months. Doubts about his path in life were eating away at his confidence like termites, and the burial was not helping.

By the time the lacquered hearse carriage was loaded with the enormous white casket holding the body of King Sugar Charmaine, the pair of white horses was fuming and fretting, and the sky made good on its early morning threats. A cold drizzle peppered the faces of the mourners exiting the oversized wooden doors of the Frank Lloyd Funeral Home. They held tightly to one another's furs, leaning into frigid Chicago winds armed with useless black umbrellas.

All the grieving, and the horses, and the smells, they were taking Twilight away from the procession and back, way back, to the red clay of Clarksdale, Mississippi, to his childhood home where it all began.

Twilight's pimp potential manifested itself on the Delta, when he still went by his real name: Cassius Mitchell. The hustler life showed up in him early on: at five years old he was tricking duller kids out of their candy, and then their toys. He was a fourth-generation outlaw, his bloodline carrying its share of gangsta on both sides, but it wouldn't be right to look into Twilight's family history and say there was a clear pattern leading up to his future lifestyle of cunning and decadence. It wouldn't be right either to say that Twilight the pimp was a bolt out of the clear blue sky. He came from good people and not-so-good people, and good people who did not-so-good things. The Mitchells and McCraes were like most Southern black folk: slavery had sharpened their survival skills, while leaving intricate psychological scars that sometimes turn keloid with each successive generation.

His mother, Gwen McCrae, Missy to all who knew her, was a beautiful redbone—part Choctaw they said, which explained the high cheekbones but not the red in her hair or the freckles that sprinkled her sculpted little nose. She got popular in her youth—too popular—and it could be rightly said that she enjoyed a certain infamy in her little corner of the Delta. By the time she moved to the black-owned hotel, her name had already had a long run on the rumor mill. She was always cozying up to trouble, always in some juke joint, bar, or other place where her reckless sensuality felt at home. She slept with cops and criminals, black and white, and had her way with all of them.

Baynard Mitchell was a rumrunner with an easy country charm about him. He had a good hustle going, so good it was almost legal. After the repeal of Prohibition, Mississippi could never make up its mind; so some counties were dry and some were wet. If you lived in a dry county you might go to one of the juke joints on the county line and buy a setup—for two bits you'd get a bowl of ice, some lemons, and a 7UP; then for another fee you'd get a bottle, and you'd best be prepared to down the whole thing, you and your party, because no one wanted you walking out the door with it. Naturally, though, there were some people in dry counties who thought this was a lot of bother and wanted to drink in the comfort of their own homes, and that's where Baynard Mitchell came in. He had a cab company in a dry county, a three-cab operation that sold sealed liquor from the cabs. Somebody would call up and order a cab, telling the young girl on dispatch to have the driver pick up a dozen eggs on the way over. A half dozen eggs was a pint of liquor; a dozen was a quart bottle. So Baynard would go to the next county, pick up a bottle, bring it to the customer, and sometimes even help him put it away—because he was friendly like that.

But most folks knew his charm had its limits and quickly gave him a nickname. They called him Rasputin, because he was quiet and charming, but he could snap a man's neck with one blow, and was known to have done it more than once. Still, according to everyone who knew him at the time, he had a civilizing affect on Missy. The blurry Polaroid taken in the spring before Cassius was born said it all. He: blood-red T-shirt and a badger-skin coat, a gold herringbone lying flat on his chest, fedora kicked ace/deuce, chewing a piece of wood between his sparkling teeth. She: standing in profile, hand on hip, head turned to the camera, strapless scarlet dress painted on, dark glasses, deep red lips on a mouth wide open.

He: one hand resting on her opposite hip, the other holding a bottle.

She: leaning against his chest with a cigarette raised in her other hand.

They met on one of his drops in Grenada. He had a side hustle shuttling corn liquor to a joint called the County Line, where Delta blues still reigned supreme even as soul ruled the day elsewhere. She liked to dance there and find company, never a big challenge. She was dancing with somebody's cousin once, a sad and dapper round man in his fifties who owned a half dozen funeral homes in Memphis and got reeled in by her on the first cast; she could have had him, could have set herself up for life and never looked back, but the moment Rasputin walked in the door she stopped still. She didn't even pretend, didn't say so much as "excuse me," just walked out of his arms and right up to Rasputin. "You feel all right, Daddy?" she said, nostrils flaring, eyes flashing, locked on his.

"Never better, baby. Why you ax?" he said, lip curling in a smile, eyes flashing right back.

" 'Cause I'm good for what ails you, Daddy. Whatsoever it is."

"Then I might be comin' down with somethin'."

He made his drop, got his cash, and took her to his place. It seemed to both of them like weeks before he ever had his dick out of her pussy for any longer than it took them to pee.

For a good minute everything was fine. Rasputin was rolling in more green than he knew what to do with. Even aside from the liquor and taxi money, he came up on the kind of dice streak that makes a man a gambling legend. In a three-month period he hit up on about $52,000. It was like he couldn't throw bad if he tried. He credited the streak to the High John the Conqueror root he walked around with—and to Missy. He was riding her around in a Chrysler convertible, mosquito wire covering the grille, and fat rolls of bills bulging in his pocket. High on life, they got married, bought a big house, and planned a future together.

But six months into the sex, liquor, and cocaine their luck turned. The dice went cold on him and his suppliers down south got knocked by the Feds. Then the relationship turned violent when the money and clothes and cars suddenly dried up.

That was when she told him she was pregnant.

Cassius's earliest memories of childhood were of his father and mother fighting, and the years of conflict between his parents stayed with him like a bullet you can't take out without killing the patient. Play a gritty copy of Al Green's "I'm Glad You're Mine," hot with pops and static, and Twilight would be shot back to 1974 and the night he found Missy knocked-out drunk with her head wet with blood where Rasputin had smacked her around. Some nights Cassius would sit outside for hours, waiting for the screaming and the furniture throwing to end.

One day it finally did: Rasputin got hit on a charge, but all Missy and young Cassius knew was that he was gone. And after a while it was Missy and Cassius sitting around a house filled with furniture, alone.

Slow desperation crept in like bad weather. His mother started to go around again, and Cassius ended up spending more time with his cousins. Folks started seeing Missy with Mo Sutton, a would-be hustler who was never without his mouth jewelry. Loud, irascible, with high highs and low lows, he came to visit more and more, until he forgot to stop visiting and just stayed. No announcement that he was moving in—he was just there.

Cassius might have been four by this time, and once when Mo was "working" he made the mistake of asking the man for some candy money. Mo, on his knees with his back turned as if in prayer, finally turned from big clumps of yellowish powder he was tending to on the naked mattress and stared down at Cassius through a cloud of pungent smoke. "Money fuh *candy*? Better go sell some dick, shiiit, g'wan!"

Cassius screwed up his little face like he was about to let loose with a good old *I hate you!* But instead he took a deep breath, turned to walk away, and as he turned said, totally matter-of-factly, "Fuck you."

Mo's eyes bugged, but by the time he jumped up to whup the boy's ass Cassius was long gone.

Cassius shuttled between his momma's and Uncle Poke's, wearing the aging clothes of better times. Mo was not the hustler he claimed to be, and Missy started day work as a maid. Uncle Poke took care of him, though. Poke lived about three miles north and owned a small five-and-dime on the main strip that also housed a tiny barbershop where Cassius did little errands for tips, running in and out, buying the customers Salems and whatnot.

One early morning he pushed into the shop for some errand work and found Poke

and Poke's girlfriend Diana sitting in the barber chairs. They sat still in the morning heat, like they were catching a catnap before the customers started coming. But flies were buzzing around their heads, and they didn't shoo them away. Their necks were slit. Poke's three-piece suit looked sweat-soaked with blood. Diana, in the next chair over, was bathed in it: her breasts had been slashed for good measure. When the first customers came in, they found Cassius touching his aunt and uncle's necks to see if the blood was real.

Cassius never found out why they were killed, not really: something about Poke being in possession of a white woman's heirloom, but not enough details to make more sense than that. What followed was warm rain, dark umbrellas, hurried funeral, clapboard church, muddy burial, and then night after night of watching his mother frantic in anticipation of some unspecified doom. She stopped going to work. She stood at the door for hours, staring through the peephole of her apartment.

"They coming for me tonight," she kept saying. "Oh Jesusjesusjesusjesus they comin' for me." He sat up in his bed, waiting for the Grim Reaper to come take Momma, and trying to think of a way to save her.

Cassius didn't know till he was grown how his uncle's death brought the heat down on her: the two had been stealing money from the government somehow. So when the frightful knock finally came it wasn't death but two well-dressed white men with a lot of questions.

"Ms. Gwen McCrae? We're with the FBI."

"Naw, I'm her sistuh," she swallowed. "I ain't seen her in weeks."

"Do you expect her anytime soon?"

"Huh! Whenever she *feel* like it!"

"Well, if you do speak with her, please tell her to give us a call. Here's my card. It's very important that we get in touch with her."

"Mm-hmm."

She looked the card over like she was memorizing the number. "But if you find the hooker first, tell her to come get her fuckin' kid!"

They thanked her politely and got back in their Chevrolet.

She waited a safe half hour, strolled down the street to make a casual phone call, and strolled back. Then she grabbed some panties, some cash, and Cassius, and lit out. Mo was waiting outside, with the Buick running and plenty of gas in the tank. They headed to Chicago, a long, hard trip. She sat in the back with Cassius most of the time, rubbing his head and whispering, "It's all gonna be all right, baby. It's all gonna be all right."

This was the first time Cassius saw, with his own eyes, his mother turn tricks. Every couple of hours they'd pull into a truck stop, Missy would say, "I'm a powder my nose," and Mo would say to Cassius, "C'mawn," almost affectionate. He'd go inside with Mo, sit at the counter and play with straws, and stare at the door waiting for Missy while Mo drank a slow cup of coffee. Every time he'd try to slide down from the chair to go find his mother, Mo would whap him on the head and tell him to stay put. Eventually she'd walk in, looking like she'd just fixed her makeup, pay for Mo's coffee, and say, "Let's go." The fifth or sixth time she took a lot longer, and Cassius was getting antsy. When Mo was staring into his coffee, he jumped down from the stool and ran out the door, saying, "Nose powder don't take *that* long!" Mo started to run but the manager yelled, "Hey, you gotta pay for that coffee!" and the delay gave Cassius the time—time to run out in the parking lot, call for his momma, and turn to the sound of muffled yelling to see her stumble down from the cabin of a big rig, no makeup on and a haze in her eyes.

He never went looking for her again.

He also saw Missy take Mo for a ride. She ditched him somewhere in Illinois, got a bus ticket, and took Cassius to stay with her people in Chicago. They lived with Missy's sister in Cabrini Green, moving unannounced and uninvited into a two-bedroom that was already overcrowded, on the eighteenth floor of a building they called the Palace. Cassius's big aunt stayed drunk more than sober, and the family was cornbread folk. They were running a welfare scam, getting two checks by having a Wisconsin address in addition to the one in Cabrini Green.

That first night Cassius went around with his youngest cousin, Sherm, only a year older than he was, but already a character: "I'm a mack, man, a mack daddy, man, call me Mack Sherm, ya understand?" Young Cassius didn't laugh at his cousin's bravado—they were only two blocks from the local track, and a kid who's seen his mother have sex with strangers for money doesn't think anything's impossible. This Chicago was a drab geometry of projects, Laundromats, liquor stores, and apostolic churches, but over the years the Chi got into him. Especially summertime: chasing dogs, guys with wingding hats and the slicked-back hairstyle they called "the butters," fried chicken and turnip greens, playing pitty-pat for pennies, the talk of murderers up the street, the giant speakers dragged out on the Fourth of July blaring summer anthems—"If you wanna ride, don't ride the white horse"—and everywhere you looked teenage, early-ripe girls and lanky boys grinding in the street. Cassius grew into Chicago and started to get comfy. He was smooth, he was good-looking, and he had what they called "mouth game" in spades.

His good looks were almost a problem though. People had fawned over him back in Clarksdale, but there was always so much drama he got pushed into the background. But now he was surrounded by aunties and girl cousins and neighbors who like to dropped their jaws the first time they saw him, falling all over themselves to say how pretty he was: his almond skin, light brown eyes, baby hair slicked back to show his widow's peak, his dimples, and the dozen or so freckles Missy had passed on to him. His cousins would fight to braid his hair at night, and fight again to comb it out in the morning. His momma and aunties kept him dressed in the latest. He kicked at first—

STREET

"Lea' me be!" "I ain't pretty!" "G'wan, git away!"—but by the time he was seven and growing like a weed, already a head taller than Sherm who was a year older, he was used to it. Matter of fact, he expected it—women doting on him just felt like the natural state of things. He never felt pretty, never *really* believed the hype, but he knew *they* did, and all he had to do was talk to a girl to seal the deal. It didn't even matter what he said, because how he said it, plus how he looked, was all it ever took.

His cousin Sherm didn't mind it because as Cassius's best friend, he was the beneficiary of spillover attention, and he always milked it for anything he could get. But some of the other boys didn't take it so lightly. When the other boys saw his pretty looks and his grooming and his clothes, they thought he might be fey. But he was such a cold and vicious fighter that by the time he got to second grade, nobody took his looks for anything but good luck.

In the Gospel According to Twilight, that's where it all began. To hear him tell it, his coming up in the game like he did was destiny. From the age of eight, Cassius was smoking, having his baby-sitters give him head, and getting pussy before he knew what to do with it. He was a player by age nine—he turned the girls on, and they would give him things: sneakers, meals, clothing, money. It became a source of income, and not extra income either, as his momma had already taken the first steps down that slow road to depression.

But it was more than ten years before he finally found a father, and that was in King Sugar Charmaine. But that was two eternities ago, and now the man was dead.

♦　♠　♥　♣

The end of Charmaine's funeral found a more sociable Twilight and a hard core of the other guests drinking in the Marquis Room. After that, still feeling restless, they all headed over to a private gathering up at the club, where some strippers were supposedly giving some kind of something in Charmaine's honor. A glittering caravan of SUVs, Coupes, and Benzes went rolling through the land: south down the west side, honking into the night, finally parking all up and down Monroe. Twilight, alcohol-eased into a warm bath of memories, got to pouring out Courvoisier in the back of his big-body Benz with his boys Sherm and Vogue and laughing about old times. There was the time they partied out in Vegas with Charmaine, a certain rap star, and a college football player turned rap entrepreneur; that one time when they turned Freaknik out with them crazy hos from Alabama; that Filipino transvestite who had almost had Vogue fooled for the better part of an hour. . . .

"We like Virginia Slims, baby," said Sherm, raising the plastic cup full to the brim with Crown Royal. "We come a long way." Then after a pause: "They sent him out right, though, in all his finery. That's love right dere."

Twilight nodded. "He earned a send-off like that. Man was like daddy dearest. They ain't gonna be another."

Vogue poured some more whiskey in his cup. "Ain't no thing, baby. Charmaine probably turnin' some big tittie angel out as we speaking here tonight, postin' her up by the pearly gates with God's permission, ya dig? The game don't stop." Twilight smiled, bumped fists with Vogue, and felt his eyes start to well up.

"Damn, my niggah—you gon' have me leaking in here like a goddamn square! Pass me that bottle, 'cause I'm 'bout to get fucked up."

# Game Still Recognize Game

For young Cassius Mitchell, his initiation into the game was so gradual it felt inevitable. School was always more a place to socialize than where he learned, and by the time he was sixteen he hadn't dropped out so much as faded out. The way he saw it, he had two options: either he was going to become a soldier with one of the gangs or he was going to get one of those young, fast girls to bring him some money. Hustling would have to turn from part-time pastime to regular business, but he wasn't ready to go all the way, and he wouldn't have known how to really get there if he *was* ready. He had a vision of himself as the kind of hustler he saw in glimpses up and down Madison like a preacher—but had no idea what it took to make that vision a reality. So the first money-making venture he stumbled onto was a job, on the line at a factory that made furniture for low-end beauty parlors.

He was barely seventeen, spending hours staple-gunning vinyl over Hollofil over pressboard, or bending a thousand angle irons to make something he would never even see. But his whole sense of himself was changing for the bigger, getting more grandiose the more his real options dwindled. He was having "a lot of necessities." The twos and fews he was getting at the factory made it hard to keep working there, and the little extra he got selling smoke to his coworkers barely paid for his other expenses. The older and taller he got, the more his momma leaned on him. After he kicked in for food and electric, and incidentals, and sneakers for his baby cousins, and this situation and that emergency, he was barely keeping up with the cost of living.

He and some of his people at the plant talked about getting out of this dead-end bullshit. He got tired of whites talking to him like he owed them something. He just wasn't meant for the nine-to-five—it wasn't him—and after seven weeks on the job, he quit. He got in one some stickup work, then some breaking and entering; he'd go up to the North end with some girls that would case a house to hit the following week, or lay for marks on the weekends. For a while it paid, but it was a funny thing: the more money he had, the less he could hold on to it. He got himself some clothes and jewelry, but he was still struggling between jobs—*Damn, seem like I was flush a day ago.* And wild and blind as he was, all the money really got him in the end was some prison time. Stopping him for a make-believe traffic violation on his way back from a B&E, the police got a nice surprise when they found about $50,000 worth of stolen goods in the trunk. He never made it to see the fence and his cousin Sherm.

Prison was like Crime Academy. He suffered the usual indignities: the guards had German shepherds sniffing at his ass, and he slaved in the kitchen for fifty cents an hour, but overall he had it easier than some, and prison made Cassius a full-out hustler. It slowed his walk, made him a loner, and after the first few months of watching the calendar go by, banging his fists on the wall in blind rage and disbelief, he learned to "jail" the rest of his time. He slept late, lay in the cut, made alliances and enemies, and got schooled in the game, in all manner of scam. He found out how to buy a car with a mix of fake and real bills, and then travel to another state and sell it for triple the money. How to oil fingers while shaking hands to slip off rings. How to psychologically corner a woman and have her do his bidding. He was also exposed to various religions, the deeper philosophy behind hustling. Everything was interesting to him—he wanted to know it all—but anything about how to work a woman for profit reached in and grabbed his heart. He felt it was something he'd already been doing, just unconsciously. Women had been giving to him his whole life, to the point where he'd taken it for granted. And now, the more his prison mates glorified the art of pimping, the more he wanted to test his newly minted skills.

Days after he got out, Cassius sat in a bar drinking when he caught a glimpse of a coffee-complexioned queen, her honey-blond hair feathered around her shoulders and down her back. Fascinated, he watched the reaction of every man she passed, before turning back to her. He saw the pretty, round ass atop strong thighs and shapely legs, and her back permanently arched. She caught him looking and turned to give him the full view. He smiled and caught the action in the bar mirror in front of him.

Before he knew it, she was standing next to him, her eyes fixed on the bartender, her hair falling over one shoulder. While she waited, he watched her figure in profile. The ass wouldn't stop calling, and the arched back sent a full-body thrill through him.

He figured she was older than he was, but he couldn't even guess by how much—two years? five? ten? fifteen? She settled that perfect bottom onto the seat beside him but never acknowledged his presence. For his part, he didn't pretend: he kept his stare locked on her, watching the way her body looked in her hugging dress, which in the darkness of the bar made her seem naked.

The bartender set down her Cosmopolitan, napkin, and glass. Cassius saw that as his cue and took care of it. He stared into the woman's eyes, almost the same light brown as her skin. And then he turned his focus to her ass. Her finish was smooth, with a sheen to it, and her arms were tatted: legs, back, and thighs.

He was so busy checking her out that he didn't realize she had spoken to him until she asked him a second time for a light. As he raised the match to the Newport, she threw back her hair, took a drag, and then started sucking on her straw. His eyes went to her nipples. Realizing she had his attention, she stuck her tongue out to show him her piercing, and he noticed the gleam of silver in her mouth.

"You like that, baby? I got two more. One I can show you, the other . . ."

She had light circles under her eyes, and it attracted him even more. It only added to her appeal. Her voice was warm and she talked like they'd known each other for years.

First thing she told him was that she'd just gotten out of the joint that day. "Three P.M. today, baby."

"You too? Fer real?! Shoo, let's drink," he told her.

He listened as she set into telling her life story. Her name was Angela and she used to be a dancer. Thirty-five years old and from Gary, "right 'round where the Jackson Five used to live. "And," she finished, "my granddaddy was a pimp, my daddy pimped, and my mom ho'd. . . . Shit, what's a ho supposed to do?!" She laughed and ordered another drink.

He kept her in the drinks and lit her cigarettes while she talked. Now that he got a closer look at her tattoos, he could make out that they were names, men's names—he figured they were the names of husbands and daddies.

She had just served three of a three-to-five for "pandering," running an operation booking girls for clients at conventions, and she never shut up. "You probably thinkin' I'm crazy, the way I'm goin' on," she said, but when he laughed she shook her head. "No, baby, I just love to talk. And I can see you lovin' to listen at me." She winked at him, laughed, and went on, giving him her whole life story in broken sentences. He liked her; she was funny and smart, and she had his full attention. He saw that the drink and conversation had melted away just about all of her inhibitions, whatever inhibitions she'd had to begin with. She started asking questions about him, and then did what Twilight had been used to since childhood—she mentioned his widow's peak, his long eyelashes, played with his shoulder-length hair, and all the while called him "baby" in a sweet, breathy voice.

"Baby, where'd you say you was from?"

She looked him up and down, sized him up. "Hmm, baby, you got something special in you. You give me a really good feeling inside." Then she nonchalantly placed her hand on his dick, took his hand, and put it between her legs. Her pussy was as warm as her voice. She smelled of Chanel and tobacco.

"Baby, who are you?" she asked him. "What do you need?"

Once they got to the room she was renting in a boardinghouse, she asked him again, "Baby, do you need something?" He reached again for the wetness between her legs.

She moaned to herself. "Hmm, Daddy, you *do* need something." She pulled away slightly to tease him with her hazel eyes and look him over.

"Niggah, what is your *name*?"

He lay a kiss on the back of her neck, turned things on, and worked the opening under her dress.

"Oh, mmm, Daddy, I need me something, too. You got something for me."

Cassius moved close up on her backside.

"Uh-huh! Oh, damn, I knew you would take care of this, you gonna work it. I know you getting it ready, yeah, that's right. Get it real wet, umm, you know what I need. . . ." And on and on and on. She talked through the whole thing, but he didn't mind: the warmth of her voice wore away at the cold inside him, freed the locked-up man in him. She was unlike any girl he'd ever been with. She was 100 percent down to be stroked.

She dropped to her knees and ran her tongue around the outline of his dick, and before he knew it, she was laying down technique—the bitch had skills. He was just trying to hold on to what cool he had left.

"Umm, been a long time . . ."

"Then quick," she said, "come over to the bed, niggah, and lay it on me." Before he knew it, she was turned around on all fours, ass out and up, and he accepted the invitation.

"Do me, Daddy," she moaned. "It's been so long. I need it! Yeah! Mmm, deep. Yeah, turn it inside out. Baby, you fucking me like you paying rent. Take it, Daddy, make me come for you!"

They fucked all night. She slept until the sun was about to rise and woke smiling. She ran her fingers through his hair. Her eyes downward, she watched him come to life again.

"You my little baby, my twilight baby." She looked out the window. "Twilight. That's what I'm a call you."

She never gave him a solid reason for the name: it was because of the hours he kept, because he could keep it going from sundown to sunup, because he came alive when it started to get dark . . . but it was different, and the more she said it, the more it sounded right.

Angela gave Twilight more than his pimp name. She brought him through the gate of a woman's mind. Living with her gave him the chance to experience the hustle from the ho's point of view, and they developed a strong bond that went beyond fucking: Angela rocked it in the bed *and* she fed his soul. Her cooking fattened him up, but even more important, she fed his mind. It was the closest thing he ever had to a real relationship. Anything more than a week seemed like marriage to him, like a lifetime, but with her, time went fast.

And she started giving him money the second day. "Start-up money," she called it. "You know, to look nice, baby." She suggested he buy clothes with it, and when he returned tailored in a gray suit, jewelry, and matching brim, smiling, and sprawling on the bed naked, she said, "Baby, I missed you."

Within two weeks she was giving him all her pay. She'd leave it on the dresser, never once asking how he was going to make a living. She only demanded that he fuck her, and that he look his sharpest.

Angela was his start-up ho. She already knew all the angles and took Twilight through his first moves. She gave him her all: whatever he wanted, she supplied him with. She was his first baby steps in the pimp/ho game and his tutor in the art of pussy hustling.

And so Twilight rose to the occasion. He drove her ride, nurtured her, and handled the money. Life in prison seemed like the middle passage to him now. To him Angela was his ticket into the promised land.

One gray afternoon they were driving. She was sucking on a Blow Pop and looking like an overripe teenage girl in the passenger's seat. "You know, Daddy," she said. "I'd rather you sell it than to give my shit away for free." She handed him a wad of bills as he pulled up in front of the club. "Even exchange is no robbery." Backing out of the ride ass-first, she disappeared into the bar to dance.

Twilight heard his given name being called out of the blue. It was his cousin Sherm coming over to the car.

"Ooh, nice ride, cuz. When did you get out?" Sherm's eyes were on the shiny exterior. He reached in to feel the leather. "Damn, niggah—you done *landed.*"

Twilight smiled, just happy to see the only family he had.

Sherm went on. "Where's your bitch at, niggah? You *must* be peddling pussy. Your threads is too sharp, playah—must cost 'bout a thousand."

Twilight grinned. "Try two." Sherm's mouth dropped open. They both broke up laughing and hugged like brothers. He brought Sherm around the Coupe and Sherm played it cool. They smoked some weed, reminisced, and talked about the future. They were seeing each other as adults for the first time and must have liked what they saw, because they started to hang again, just like they did when they were boys. Later they picked up Angela and went to Madame X's to get nice. The three of them became regulars.

Sherm became Twilight's direct line to the streets. Everybody knew Sherm through him running numbers, but now he was ready to get in the ho game. He had a girl of seventeen he was about to put on a corner—said she had an itch and he was gonna help her scratch it. Sherm had started to develop a style of his own. He cut the figure but was still just trying to come up in the game. As Sherm worked his way into the game, Twilight was just trying to keep Angela under control.

After a couple of months of tension her behavior started to get out of hand, and one day she got in her drink and let it fly. They sat at Marty's, and she got so wild Twilight slapped her to save face.

"Who the fuck is you?" she snapped back. "I'm not your wife. I'm a ho." He didn't say a word, but before he could have, she kept going, "Yeah, niggah, what?" She wagged her finger in his face, and then pointed to her pussy. "You think this is yours? This is mine, motherfucker." Twilight pushed her outside toward the car, but before he could get in, she slid over behind the wheel defiantly. He looked at her and slowly pulled the key out of his pocket, shaking his head. He wondered how a grown woman could be so childish.

*She needs a good ass-beating*, he thought, but then he thought again. He was gonna reckon with her the way she had taught him. From that point on, he denied her what she wanted most: affection.

From that night on, their lives took separate directions. Angela moved in on Sherm, playing on his greed. Twilight pulled out of their way, found his own space, and disappeared. *She wants to move on, so let her,* he thought. *Sherm wants to be in my shoes so bad, let him. A real pimp doesn't waste time with simpleminded shit.* Still, he wasn't a real pimp, not yet anyway, and he knew it.

A prison connect quickly got him work at Jumbo's, a nearby pool hall. Twilight worked the front, watching as various pimps, gangsters, dealers, hustlers, and slum kings came to play nine ball and gamble in Jumbo's back room. Men like Price, Absolute, and Garfield played in uniform, full minks and hats, and their lives put flesh on his fantasies. One night he saw Garfield bring in one of his finest hos on a dare—a pink-eyed albino whose tattoos, along with her black bra and panties, burned bright on her alabaster skin—and with the slightest gesture Garfield could make her shake her pretty naked ass on the red pool table.

It took Jumbo about an hour to calm the place down.

Their displays of machismo and control fed Twilight's hunger. Seeing Garfield's trophy shaking her ass and watching him execute a pimp's control over her every move made him crave the game like he'd never craved before. He knew now he had to put everything else down, everything aside, and grab one of those crowns. In his mind there was no question that he was born to pimp. The only question was how to start.

◆   ♠   ♥   ♣

Twilight spent most of his time with Tango, a veteran player who was pushing eighty but could *still* knock a bitch if he wanted to. He had a voice like a rusty motor, and most of the time drank Old Crow and played poker in the back room. Old hustlers tend to fade away like old soldiers, legends in their own minds, but it's a long slow fade to black; most are a vague, bitter presence in the streets, becoming building doormen if they're

lucky, otherwise floating in and out of the bars and liquor stores, pathetic as one-hit won-ders who think they're still stars. But Tango was a player of a different kind. He'd had at least a hundred hos in his life, and he still enjoyed his women and his music: old-school gods like Johnny "Guitar" Watson, Muddy Waters, Junior Walker. And he'd *still* jack at hos, just for the sport of it—he called it nonprofit pimping. But despite his shadowy vocation Tango stayed clean. Clean as the board of health. He'd deck himself out in full-length leather trenches, herringbone suits, fedoras, and such—and not vintage vines, either, but this year's model. He said he had but one vice, one addiction, and that was clothes.

Tango recognized something in Twilight—a kindred spirit, maybe, or the makings of a natural—and he was brimming with warnings and barbed encouragements about the life. "You won't even know you're trapped, young blood, 'til it's too late. But you could be more. You got a predator's eye. Get your shit tight and you could be the greatest. After me, of course." The old man told outrageous lies about his women and his exploits, his schemes and his ploys; funny thing was, the most outlandish tales were true. Most of the cats in the pool hall figured he was crazy, brains getting soft. Jumbo guessed it was from so many years in the joint. But Twilight peeped game. True, most things he said Twilight could barely follow, but Tango had his moments, beautiful lucid moments where he schooled young Twilight tuition-free.

"I spent a dozen years in and out of prison," he might start. "I was a repeat offender, but I was always a contender. I never had a black juror in any of my cases, but I never served time for a crime I didn't commit." Inside the joint, Tango became a jailhouse lawyer. He studied oratory, memorizing and reciting long passages from anyone who sounded good—Oscar Wilde, Napoleon, it didn't matter. "I realized things when I was in that labyrinthine hell," he'd say, "under the goddamn din of the prison keeping me up, I could hear that clanging and them voices in my goddamn dreams. We was dead men, Pops, all dead men slowly getting digested in the belly of Leviathan. But I was able to rise up out of its jaws with the power of my mind and voice. Do you know I sued the prison system thirty-one times? They had to let me go."

Twilight would be cleaning up or collecting the pool sticks and Tango would drop a snippet of sage counsel in passing: "See, a king is a man who knows the truth and the truth has set him free. He is the word manifest." Another night he might blow heavy.

"If you gonna do this thang, live from the womb, or any venture for that matter, do it to win. Aspire to be a true, live gentleman scholar and king because, see, this is not a physical matter, son. It's a skull game. A gorilla can only get but so far beating bitches into submission. To control a woman's body you must first control her mind. If a girl come to you looking for direction, become her director. All these nobodies callin' themselves pimps and players, why it's a gottdamn shame. These niggahs out here don't know how to *spell* player. Time was, it was about elegance—there used to be codes and precise etiquette. Now it's bullshit—busters and suckers who couldn't be a fly on the shit of a king pimp like Baby Bell! Now there was a true player in this game. He had white bitches at his beck and call. A true player. . . ."

And once he sensed that Twilight was seriously looking to pimp, he wouldn't stop. One night: "It's one thing to let a ho be a ho. It's another to turn a bitch out. Always know exactly who you bringin' into your family. Always do the math before you make any move. A bullshit broad not handled right can bring you down. Mind what I tell you, and just walk away—you might be slicker than today but you ain't smarter than tomorra. The game takes prisoners. And if you fall in love, give it up, because this game is about the money, not the honey. All your girls is freelancing. Some come to play, others come to pay, but none of them come to stay. . . ."

He took a long swallow of Old Crow. "But if you want to make the stay worth your while and worth the trouble, you got to hypnotize her. You hear me, boy? You be a caveman and drag her in by the hair, kicking and screaming bloody murder, you'll pay for it, no matter how much you beat her down. Don't be a troglodyte—use *pimpnosis* on the bitch, put her in a hypnotic state, draw her in by the brain and leave her hypmatized, mesmerized, *pimpnotized.*"

For Twilight this was all good, but it was still all talk, words to file away while he was still unknowing. He kept a pretty girl by his side, but he wasn't put up on real game, wasn't out there in the thick of things. . . until that fateful trip where he finally got his hands dirty. Vegas.

♦   ♠   ♥   ♣

He overheard a few of the players at the pool hall talking about going to the middleweight title match out at Caesar's Palace. Something told him to go even though one, he was violating his parole, and two, he didn't have his money tight like that. He got a round-trip ticket anyway, some gear, and went anyhow.

Vegas was a trip. The strip was an inferno of flashing neon and clanging slot machines. The legions of the old and the lame who normally filled the decrepit life of the town were pushed aside to make room for the star-studded fight crowd. It was Twilight's first glimpse of the elite criminal class who were running with the money. High rollers strolled from casino to casino flashing heavy knots and ready to spend like it wasn't no thing. The criminal elite mingling with Hollywood mingling with sports legends mingling with international players and hustlers.

Twilight recognized some of the cats from the pool hall, like Garfield and Price. They were happy to see him making moves so young, gave him the layout, and confirmed a hierarchy among hustlers that he had only a vague sense of back in the Chi, and it was very different from the pecking order in the joint, where drug kings and thugs ruled the roost. Out here, counterfeiters, paper players, cannons, and fakes were near the top, alongside macks, true macks. Players were lower, plain old pimps were way lower—maybe the same level as boosters and till tappers—and of course at the bottom was the streetwalker, along with other no-skill trades like strong-arm, stickup, and B&E. Twilight was learning. He watched the professional pickpockets working the pre- and postfight crowds; he saw that sneak thieves weren't the same as second-story men, and so on. Each had his place and got a different level of respect.

The fight-night air at Caesar's was electric. It was a playground with glittering amusements fit for a king. Every moment brought some kind of exclusive surprise, or unpredictable beauty, or sly, witty words spoken in the secret language of the ghetto elite. It was all new to Twilight. He had never seen nor heard of anything like it before. It hit him that, with just a few exceptions like Garfield and Price and maybe old Tango, the squares he thought were players were mostly impostors doing little more than chili pimping, perpetrating frauds in loud, gaudy outfits. But these muthafuckahs out here in Vegas were a different breed entirely, they were high frequency, doing it at full speed.

The fight itself was historic. For fans, maybe the most incredible spectacle of speed, strength, and heart ever seen. Tommy "the Hit Man" Hearns and Marvelous Marvin Hagler went toe-to-toe in a blur of force and will. Blood streamed from a gash on Hagler's face and for a moment it seemed Hearns had won it. But when they got back to banging, Richard Steele stopped the fight when Hagler dropped Hearns in the third round.

The postfight was festive, carnival-like. Twilight spent most of his time perfecting his craft, sharpening his tongue on freelance hos almost as new to the game as he was. But he was also steadily watching the various operations move on the moneyed crowd.

Twilight bumped into Price and one of his women, Peaches. Price wore bug-eyed glasses and a jewel-covered sombrero; Peaches was in a tiny dress covered with beads that matched. After they copped some weed from Twilight, Peaches told him that some of them were headed over to Binion's Horseshoe to gamble and that Twilight was welcome to join them.

Up at Binion's, Price introduced Twilight to a motley collection of the younger up-and-comers, among them Red, an effeminate Napoleon cat from St. Louis, draped head-to-toe in burgundy. Red looked Twilight up and down, and immediately went to testing him.

" 'Ey, buy me a drink," Red said, looking straight into Twilight's eyes.

Twilight looked back, cool and calm. "I think you've mistaken me for somebody else."

Price saw what was going on and headed it off at the pass. "Red, I got yuh. What you drinkin'? Drinks for all my people, bartender!"

Twilight had no trouble making friends with some of the others, and for a good chunk of the night they roamed the casino in a small pack, talking and laughing and throwing back a candy-sweet but potent drink called Player's Passion. The rim of a martini glass was trimmed with pure cane granules, and the contents were a blend of Midori, lemon Absolut, and Alizé Red, all shaken not stirred, of course, to make a glowing turquoise elixir, set off with a red straw and an orange umbrella.

Round about three A.M. Price went over to the roulette table, but before he did he pulled Twilight aside slowly but smoothly. "Watch your back," he said out the side of his mouth, looking over his glasses. "That Red be hatin' like a baby momma."

"I'm already knowin'. He looked at me like I did him somethin'."

"Just keep it cool, playah, but stay on ya toes." Price winked at him.

Like he was waiting for his cue, Red sauntered up and invited Twilight to some of the private games upstairs. Maybe he pegged Twilight as a vic or figured he could make some quick ends from someone so green in the game, but regardless, Twilight followed.

In the crowded elevator on the way up, Twilight confirmed his hunch that although Red was a small man, he had some gorilla in him when he turned on his ho Nakala.

"I'm really tired, Red," she whispered next to him in a hoarse voice. "I'm hungry. Let me go back to the room. The last thing you need is for me to get knocked." She was pleading.

"Naw, naw! The *last* thing I need is a bitch that's out-of-pocket! What that mean to me?" he shouted, clearly showing out for the audience. "You done lost you fucking *mind*?" He pushed his finger into her skull and she whimpered. "And stop eyeballing me like I won't bash your head in!"

She hung her head down and nodded like a child.

"Yeah, bow down to a pimp! Now get to fuckin' and suckin', bitch, and do your ho duty!"

He turned his back, stepped in front of her, and fixed his brim. For a moment no one said a word. Then a few picked up their conversations like they hadn't heard or seen a thing.

Red, Twilight, and Nakala walked into a dimly lit suite on the top floor, where a dozen or so rollers were convening around a large green table, and a couple dozen more stood nearby or sat at the smaller tables against the wall for onlookers. A game was already rolling and from the look of the chips, an accountant-looking man with no joy in his eyes was robbing the rest of these cats blind. Nakala began to circulate, while Red and Twilight sat at one of the smaller tables and ordered a drink each.

That's when Twilight got his first glimpse of King Sugar Charmaine.

Sugar was posted up in the corner, watching the game in a white mink coat with a matching brim, massive rings on his fingers, a single gold cable hanging from his neck, shoes in chartreuse and sage green on his feet. With him stood a tall sleepy-eyed blonde in a disappearing dress and boots to match Charmaine's gators.

As he took languid draws from a Dunhill in a long black holder, Twilight tried to get a read on him but couldn't; Sugar's eyes were dead silent.

When it came time, Red and Twilight sat down, and Twilight looked at the other opponents feeling confident yet cautious. Watching and playing in Jumbo's back room all that time had prepared him, but he wasn't sure he could trust the feeling. Everybody but the accountant seemed readable, still, he knew he was ass-betting—all the money he had in the world was stacked in chips in front of him: three white-and-blue, two black-and-yellow, seven slate-colored, and a dozen green. After that he had nothing but a ticket home.

They were only using three decks, and that made it possible to count cards. Twilight didn't know why they would allow that, but it didn't help him much. He won the first three hands, then bled away half his stack. But for some reason he felt good about things, figuring he had as good a chance of winning as any player at the table. An old man named Low who had the most chips started muscling the board, calling in every time he was sure. But he did it one too many times and the accountant caught him with a seven-high straight. Low had a pair of kings and it restored the balance of power some, but it did nothing for Twilight.

From the corner of his eye, he could see Charmaine watching his movements throughout the game. Eventually he came back to a couple thousand better than even, but nothing compared to the lucky streak Red was on toward the end, and Red was rubbing it in.

"Hos ain't with you tonight, huh?" Red laughed.

Twilight's blood rushed hot through him.

"You know what, Red?" he said, "I'm going for broke. I'll put everything I got on this next hand. I'm all in, against me leaving with your girl over there." Twilight pointed to Nakala, who nearly spit up her drink. Red threw back his head and laughed, but the air in the room got tight. "My bitch? Nakala? That's some shit! You want me to bet my bitch," he said laughing. "I knew your little green ass was tryna knock my bitch, mutha-fuckah, but this bitch is like American Express—I don't leave home without her. 'Sides, you ain't got the cash to equal what this pussy makes in one night, and sheee by the looks of you, son, you wouldn't know what to do with her nohow!"

At that, Charmaine walked over to the table, smiling. "I'll put the money up, son. Thirty Gs enough for ya? Count 'em." He dropped three stacks of Benjamins on the table.

The air tightened up.

Twilight looked up at Charmaine, who went back and sat down in the corner. He wasn't smiling anymore though, and Red tried to conceal his surprise.

"All right, player. You need a sponsor, I play your little bet. Deal the cards." The other players sat back and watched what was turning into a duel as the dealer passed the cards. The flop came Q♥, 6♣, 8♥.

"Come on, player. What's up your skirt? Throw 'em down!" demanded Red.

"Six titties," Twilight said with a straight face, unveiling the Q♠, Q♣.

Red threw down a pair of sixes, disgusted. He stood up as the room started snickering, and some people laughed out loud.

Nakala placed her hand playfully on Twilight's shoulder, but her eyes remained fixed on Red.

"You got it, man," Red said under his breath. Something about the way he said it made Twilight feel funny, like it was a movie and those were famous last words.

Twilight pushed Nakala's hand back toward Red.

"Keep your bitch," he said cool and calm. "I don't need her. We just playing the game." Nakala looked confused.

"Bitch, come here!" Red shouted as Nakala lowered her eyes. "Go to the room. What the fuck do you think this is, a game show, ho?!"

People started to laugh, watching as Red backed away from the table. He turned and bumped a waitress who was bringing drinks. His suit got soaked with brandy-and-cremes. The hoots and hollers got louder, and he rushed out of the room without meeting another pair of eyes.

Twilight pushed away from the table, dizzy with relief. But when he turned to thank the man who'd come to his rescue and return the money, Charmaine was gone.

Later that night, Twilight was downstairs in the casino, telling the story to a couple a cats he knew from Jumbo's, when the tall sleepy-eyed blonde brought over a bottle of Moët. She pointed to Charmaine, who raised his glass.

Twilight excused himself, walked over to Charmaine, gave him a pound. "Perfect timing. I don't know why you did that, but I'm glad you did, and I'm real relieved I didn't lose your money. Let's go over to the cage and claim your paper."

"You got heart, young blood. I like that. I believe in that, you dig? Checked with my people and they got good things to say."

"Glad to hear it. But, uh, I never got your name."

"King Sugar Charmaine. Call me Sugar. Why don't you come to the club tonight and pay me back with that bomb-ass weed I hear you totin' around? Besides, most of those bills was counterfeit." He laughed and gave him a pound, knocking his big rings on Twilight's knuckles.

It was around 5:30 when Charmaine sent his man around to pick up Twilight. He was driven from Binion's through the desert to the upscale section of Vegas. The car rolled through the gate and around the driveway to the front of the house. The manicured grounds impressed him. It was a far cry from what he knew. The house was a three-story white villa. Classic cars lined the driveway on his far right. He noticed a four-car garage, the open door displaying Charmaine's full collection of rides: a turquoise Thunderbird convertible looking brand-new, a silver Benz, and a midnight-blue Cadillac.

He was greeted at the front door by a brown-skinned *Essence* type, fine as hell, in a pinstripe suit with a short skirt. She introduced herself, looking him up and down.

"I'm Valerie . . . come in, please. . . . Our Sugar's been expecting you. Can I get you something, a drink?"

Twilight's eyes took in the expanse of Charmaine's parlor. The space was done up in shades of gray, beige, and white, a camel-colored modular pit dominating the palatial living room. A fifty-two-inch wide-screen TV stood against a wall. In the far background, he could make out a few guests lying around a lit pool through the French windows that lined the room. The living room was filled with trophies, books, photos, and large paintings in heavy gold frames. One piece of artwork in particular caught the young man's eye, a lithograph sheet of currency, hundred-dollar bills.

Valerie excused herself.

"Please wait here while I go get Sugar."

Twilight turned to catch a glimpse of her, and Charmaine was right there.

"Twilight, my man, how's it going? Catching up on the woman's movement, I see."

"Yeah," Twilight said, a little embarrassed.

Charmaine laughed and the two knocked fists. Charmaine was wearing a sharp linen suit. His hair was slicked back and waved like something out of the Roaring Twenties. Dangling from each wrist was a gold slave bracelet with gold link chains. A matching gold chain lay at his neck.

A Japanese girl entered the room with a fine ass and sexy walk. Twilight did his best

to concentrate on the conversation while catching a glimpse. She mixed drinks, set them down, bowed slightly, and left.

"Please feel free to enjoy the show. That's Tomiko. She's from Osaka."

"I see . . . Can you speak Japanese?" he asked Charmaine.

"You know I speak three languages—English, money, and honey. I met her right here in Vegas. She's my little chimama."

"Bottom ho." He winks. "Takes care of everything. I got seven girls," Charmaine explained. "One for every day of the week."

Twilight shook his head. "Man, you got yourself a stable," his eyes drifting to Sugar's jewelry.

"I'll tell you why I wear these," Sugar offered, noticing him. "I had them made custom in Chi when I was leaving, as mementos of the passage—a reminder to never forget the past." He took a sip of his drink and nodded his head like he was watching clips from a movie of his life.

"See, I was a square in the game early. Every man has to fight the bondage of being like everybody else, and I beat that one right at the start. But then I also had to break free of the bondage of being turned out on my own shit." He leaned in close to Twilight. "Man, never be the chooser, always be the chosen. That's the difference between being a square and being a pimp. See, a smart motherfucker learns how to flip the game. Addiction is the central nervous system of what we call 'the life'; addiction can be a pimp's best friend—so long as it ain't his own!"

Twilight hung on the man's every word. Charmaine held forth while drawing four lines of powder on a mirrored tray. He rolled a C-note and passed it to Twilight, sniffing a little from his elongated pinkie nail.

"Junkies, man. They made me what I am—which is one very rich man." He threw back his head and laughed. "That's all a trick is, is a junkie. He just done fallen to pussy 'stead a blow, that's all. The ho is the tool and the pussy is his drug, his antidepressant. They say, 'love is a bitch'? Well it's true like a motherfucker," he said reaching for his glass. "Get to know that in this game. It's about knowledge, Twilight. Get your Ph.D. in this game because knowledge is a beautiful thing."

Twilight asked him what he did with his day, how he filled the time. Charmaine laughed again.

"I don't do shit. I divert myself with young talent as you see. I get rubdowns, watch TV, go shopping, and drive around. You could be doing this, too, son. I see you're hungry for game."

Charmaine sat across from him, reaching for a photo album on the table. He put it in front of Twilight and began flipping through it.

"I came up in the Chi, too."

Charmaine told him about his past, showed him pictures from the fifties, photos from his childhood, his teenage years on the street. But the pictures that fascinated Twilight the most were those of him in his twenties and thirties, Polaroids of Charmaine posing next to cars and pretty girl after pretty girl. Some of the girls were naked, some just without tops, but all looking into the camera, lying on shag rugs, and ever so often there would be an elaborately set up photo of one of his girls lying next to his name spelled out in money, "Sugah." The photos must have been taken in every hotel room across the country and overseas. Charmaine stopped at one of his Japanese girls.

"Tomiko is my ghetto geisha. You know a woman like that in Japan—pale skinned, small lips, those eyes—brings a high price. She's top of the line, but it's more than the looks with Tomiko. As with all my girls, what got me about her was her mind. In Japan a chimama is a girl that brings the clients in, and Tomiko was working with one of the best hostess clubs in Ginza, the most expensive area in Tokyo. When I met her in Vegas, she'd flown in some clients for gambling and girls. These particular Japanese business-men preferred blondes and blacks, that's how we hooked up. I saw possibilities in her. She wanted to up her game to mama-san, so I offered to bring her in. She brought her clients and we merged. Now you know out here the game is different. So we do escorts. Look at this fine motherfucker here."

He pointed to a picture of a blond girl.

"That's Ingrid—she's out by the pool right now. That's my French girl. She used to dance in Paris. We met in Hawaii. She does rubdowns, full-body works. Bad bitch! Make your eye roll back. She was a showgirl and did porno, the whole nine. And you met Valerie. Man, that broad is sharp—she crunches numbers, handles the books. I picked her up in Atlanta, took her from behind a bank counter. She was nothing but a teller back then, but she's handled my money for three or four years and I've never had a problem with her."

Twilight looked him in the eye. "And they never give you any trouble?"

Sugar met his stare. "Trouble? Hell, yeah—they wouldn't be bitches if they didn't. But nothing too crazy. Personally, I like to avoid women who ain't playing with a full deck. The key is to get yourself hos that are sexually attracted to money. We're like bees: we *extract* the honey. You wanna build a reputable female franchise, you have to master the art of suggestion. Touch a woman the right way and she's yours for life. Look into the game and see it for what it is. All women are rent to own! The line between a housewife and a ho is thin, my man."

Twilight shook his head, laughing, trying to soak it all in.

Charmaine laughed with him. "See, in many respects this is matrimony. A pimp just changes the vows. For example, I suggest you hold on to the honor and obey part; it works to your benefit, ya dig? Steer your ho toward obeying the love and protect part of the

agreement and you're set. Of course these days everything's changed in the game. The game itself is almost extinct, with all these freelance motherfuckers doin' it out of home offices. So, what's a pimp gonna do except change with the times? Shit, even this old dog had to learn some new tricks. These days it's all bogus," he said, wrapping his nails around a nectarine and taking a bite.

"It's like the men are women and the women are the new men." Just then a young girl walked in, a big round-eyed beauty with short hair and skinny legs.

"Ah, this is a female friend of mine," he said with a sly smile, "a little *surprise* for you."

"Ooh is this him, Sugar?" she said. "You was right."

"You like him, Irene?"

Irene smiled, walked over, and sat in Twilight's lap. She took his hand and Twilight looked back at Charmaine. "Go on," he said. "You family now. Irene will put you on, player." Twilight could hear Charmaine and his cronies laugh as Irene pulled him toward a series of doors beyond the game room.

Twilight didn't know what to do but follow Irene's ass as she led him into a dimly lit bedroom.

After a few minutes' chitchat and more drink, Irene stood in front of him.

"You're gonna be my daddy now," she said. "Tell me to put the money on the dresser."

Twilight was hesitant. "Put that money on the dresser," he said softly. She took her top off, pulled some money out her bra, and placed it on the dresser.

"Tell me to come over there."

A crooked line made its way across his face. "Bring that fine ass over here."

"I'm yours now," she said. "Now fuck me like you mean it."

And he did.

Afterward, when the sun was coming up and he was taking a long, deep pull off a cigarette, Irene mumbled something, and her voice bothered him. Her moans were dried up and cracked, he thought, like there was something missing inside her. In her sleep she started to look regular, less glamorous, even a little broke down. He could see the imperfections, he could smell the toll the life was taking on her—squeezing out of her.

All his senses were magnified, and every nerve ending was wide awake and reporting for duty. He was nervous, maybe even a little frightened. He went into the bathroom and stared at the mirror for a long time, looking into his own reddened eyes and wondering what had just happened, what door had just slammed shut behind him.

There was a knock on the door. It was Charmaine.

"Hey, young blood," he said. "We headed over to the casino to see what's what. You still got legs?"

"I'll be out in a minute."

"My man."

Irene stirred. He washed up, threw on his clothes, and looked again at the money. Eleven hundred dollars. He put it in his pocket and headed out, dark thoughts vanishing from his mind.

# From the Root
# to the Fruit

Under Sugar Charmaine's wing, Twilight became the latest in an unbroken imperial line of true players, men in the ruthless pursuit of status, distinction, and above all the almighty dollar. This particular lineage traced back to the Louisiana plantations, back to one Mr. Elijah Aarons. According to the stories, Elijah hustled his way off the plantation and a life of sharecropping through guile and invention. Elijah founded a bawdy house up in Canada and ran numbers in the most unlikely places—like Newport, Rhode Island. He was a scientist of the game, and his game was advanced for its time and place. He recognized that emancipation did nothing to kill white men's desire for sex with their former slaves. That recognition helped Elijah acquire land, horses, and power. He traveled up and down the Mississippi, sometimes with two

or three ladies at a time, sometimes looking to recruit. On two separate occasions he had to hightail it out of town to avoid lynch mobs. He was beyond most white folks' nightmare of the "uppity niggah"—he wasn't above breaking a bottle over a white man's head—and he could talk his way out of just about any situation. He had good instincts, and he knew that sometimes you have to sacrifice to come out ahead.

And as with all things in nature, game begets game: Elijah, over many years, traveled with and explained his hustle to a Mozell Radley from Ohio. Mozell did the same with his young cousin Miles. Miles ran with Detroit Slim, a drummer, zoot-suiter, and ladies' man. The fair-skinned Slim, a dead ringer for Adam Clayton Powell Jr., was an elegant hustler and sometimes numbers runner who worked everywhere from St. Louis to Philly, always with a number of girls who brought him street proceeds on a weekly basis. He opened a Slim's Bar back in Detroit and did well for himself, until a politician was found shot to death in one of his upstairs apartments.

Then there was Slim's protégé, Benny Campbell. Benny died in a "conflict" with the police at the St. Regis Hotel, a case that made front-page news in 1959. Before that, he spent most of his time with his favorite cousin, Lonnie Charmaine. Benny loved Lonnie, enough to bring him along on some of his excursions to Los Angeles and Harlem, giving him clothes and money to mix in, and pulling his coat on all types of hustles to earn some of his own money. Lonnie would hide behind panels in run-down hotel rooms and rifle through pockets after one of Benny's girls had fucked a john to sleep. It wasn't long before Lonnie took to pimping on his own, and by the time he was seventeen, he had five girls working for him in two towns. They called him "Sugar" due to his penchant for candy and "King Sugar" once he established himself in the game.

King Sugar Charmaine laid it out for Twilight, his new apprentice in the game, as it had been laid out for him, all up the generations of forepimps going back to Elijah. So it's no mystery that Twilight's name came to ring bells all across the country the way it did. All Twilight did was execute the cold-blooded game that was passed mouth to ear through the decades, from horsebacks to Cadillacs.

Twilight had two stallions to start: Irene, the professional booster, well trained and highly skilled, and Rebecca, a flatback ho. They worked well together and brought in steady confetti, as Charmaine gave him what amounted to a scholarship in the game. That plus his winnings in Vegas put a battery in his back, convincing Twilight that pimping was his destiny.

"You *already* pimpin'," Charmaine explained that night in Vegas. "You's a pretty muthafuckah, and a ho will do whatever you ask her to—it's just about cultivating the heart to ask. As for most of the rest, the ho will show you the way."

He was right; Irene taught him the ropes. And with her serving as bottom, Twilight began to travel across the continental United States. He didn't return to Chicago for weeks. Under Sugar's now-and-again tutelage, he attended the big events, stayed in contact with other players of his pedigree, and generally kept it popping. He picked up women all across the country and lost them almost as quickly as he got them. (One woman stole thousands from her husband to keep "a Twilight in her life.") But Twilight stuck to the player's code: he never went with a square woman. That was a violation to the working girls whose dedication and devotion he demanded and depended on. If a woman wasn't ready to ho up, wasn't nothing he could do for her.

Green as he was, pimping was treating Twilight right. His hos didn't bring in less than $4,000 large a week. Each could work from rooms he set them up in if the track (the stretch of pavement they normally walked) got too hot. Fact was, he generally avoided the track and only brought girls over if he was breaking a bitch in or, if he was low on cash, as a last resort. He preferred to work the clubs and hotels, and, unlike some of his peers, he didn't take just any ho—he liked his flatbacks clean and innocent-looking. It made it easier to work certain spots frequented by tricks with real cash. And if worse came

to worst and things got high and dry, he could always bring his girls to Atlanta or St. Louis or back to Vegas.

Cuffing new broads was a matter of maintaining the business. Subtlety was key. He would spend hours cultivating the soft curls that fell down his neck, going to the Sir George in downtown Chicago, the man who created the Superfly hairstyle. For special occasions he would style his hair into ocean waves. He showered and changed three times a day, and kept his nails on both hands and feet glossed and manicured. If there was anything Charmaine taught him, it was that pimp is in the details.

But what really gave Twilight his edge was his understanding. He spent most of his time listening. Watching. He knew a lot about the human animal. He watched the response to new things, luxurious things, things that sparkled and fed the ego. Everybody loved a winner and he was always willing to be that. He saw what the life did to a body and could tell when a ho was ready to leave or was turning into a management problem.

Trouble was unavoidable. But Twilight saw it as the price of the life. The cops were always a problem. They hated pimps and took every opportunity to harass him and reassert their own manhood in front of his girls. There were, of course, the cops who befriended him, grabbed on his girls, got their dicks wet without paying, then would double back and bust them. He tried to take their harassment in stride, making jokes and dropping logic in the face of their rabid hatred of him, because most of the time they were tripping. One cop in Georgia smashed in his windows and lights and took him in for traffic violations. He noticed how in certain places cops would allow the white girls to work the track freely but bust the black girls without mercy. They were easier on black transvestites and gay hos than they were on black girls, for reasons too deep to guess at.

One time a cop was taking him in on a trumped-up charge, and they had a long conversation in the squad car.

"Why you bringing me in on this bullshit, man?"

"It's my duty," the cop said. "You're a threat to my children."

"I ain't no threat to your children, man. You know what goes on out here. Your children in school?"

"Yes."

"Your children got values? They got they momma and they daddy?"

"Yes."

"Ain't nobody out here that ain't forced to be out here by circumstance. If these hos had home guidance they wouldn't be needing street guidance."

"That's what kills me. You out here taking advantage of these vulnerable minds, these innocent . . ."

"Where you get 'innocent' from? Listen, man, this here is by choice, not by force. Don't nobody do what they don't want to do."

"That's a load of crap. I pick up girls with blood running from their eyes, who don't even know their own names or where they come from. Don't tell me they're not forced to sell they bodies so you can ride around in fancy cars."

"I can't speak for another man," Twilight said. "I'm telling you how *I* live, and I don't beat bitches. That ain't the player way."

"The player way?" The cop turned full around. "Who sold you that bullshit? Who turned your mind around to the point that you're living by some shit called 'the player way'?"

"You ain't no player, so I wouldn't expect you to understand."

"You're right, I ain't no player. I'm a man. I live according to truth. I fear God. You, you're a player going to prison and living off young girls."

"If you so living by the truth, why ya gotta trump up charges to lock me up? The truth is that all you motherfuckers is righteous when it's convenient. Y'all lie, cheat, and steal more than niggahs on the street. Be real, man. That Bible bullshit holds no weight with me."

The cop laughed and shook his head. "You got an answer for everything, don't you?"

"That's my job."

"Well, you're going to find that you don't know everything one day, and these choices you're making are gonna catch up to you. And when you're not trying to show your hos how bad you are, that Bible will be a comfort because God loves everybo—"

"Unh-uh!" Twilight snapped. "Save the preachin' for a niggah that give a fuck, man."

His life became a rapid succession of numbers. His phone number changed constantly. His movements created a river of dates, airline reservations, credit-card numbers, fake social security numbers, bail money, area codes, counts of larceny, badge numbers. And he slowly learned over time to master those numbers and everything they represented. Played the numbers and read the dream books, a habit he picked up from his mother. Thirteen was his lucky number. He avoided fours and eights. It made him somewhat superstitious, but he looked at such things like he looked at everything else: it was a tool, not a rule.

He picked that one up from cousin Sherm. It was Sherm who first introduced him to the *idea* of the life, his first day in the Chi, and even if they weren't always side by side, in a way they came up together in the game. Wasn't so long ago you could find them in a parking lot by Marty's or the Alibi or the Marquis Room politicking with the locals, working their girls, leaning on Fleetwoods and Eldorados. Leather interiors with the piping, wood paneling, snotty grilles with the brains blown out.

Sherm wasn't the natural Twilight was, but he had a style of his own. So black he was blue, he moved and talked like the vampire he was. He capped his canine teeth in gold, greased his hair down in a style he called "Black Superman," and generally kept his look somewhere between gothic and baroque, wearing sashes, frills, capes, and whatnot. He scared his girls and treated them dirty, so he had a high turnover, even for pimping. Most of his girls were white and what pimps called "work." They were tawdry-looking hos, but they kept him in minks and finger rocks. Sherm made it to all the big events, wrists froze the fuck out, and was in on anything like funds was limitless.

But while Twilight sought the three basics—money, power, and respect—Sherm's motivation wasn't half so clear. He wanted his name to ring bells from state to state, but sometimes he'd get into dark moods that would leave him incapacitated and shut in for weeks. Twilight would find him at home, the place a pigsty, with newspapers everywhere, week-old food rotting on the table, and Sherm looking not much better. A day or two later Sherm would shave and shower, and pick up where he left off like he'd never been gone.

They went about the business of laundering their money together, first opening a garage to house their cars and bring in some legit money, then a jewelry store, and finally a Western Union. Outside of the drama that naturally came with their women, they spent most their time cultivating bigger dreams. Neither one expected the other to give him something for nothing, but each of them knew the other one had his back. They joked that they were the Butch and Sundance of the life.

◆    ♠    ♥    ♣

One night, Chicago.

Twilight, Irene, and a new girl from New Orleans, Remy, were sitting in the Cadillac preparing for work that evening. Irene was repacking her things: a half dozen tampons, cigarettes, mace, condoms, K-Y jelly, her phone, a lighter.

"Pass me some of that bottle of Crown in the back," Twilight instructed.

Remy pulled a bottle off the car floor. It turned out empty. "We out."

"That's a tragedy."

"And we should get gas now, too," Remy said, "so we don't have to get it later."

Irene looked Remy over. "Remy, you a mess. Gimme your bag."

Twilight suddenly noticed a spot on Remy's pink, see-through dress. "Damn, Remy! What the fuck is that? Shit, like dealing with a little kid." Remy, mortified, first tried to rub it out, then covered it with her hair.

Twilight, fuming, stopped at a filling station. "Go on in and get some gas in this car."

"What?"

"Go on and pump the gas."

"I'll pay for it. I don't wanna pump."

"Bitch, this ain't no game. Play your position and I'll play mine! Git, bitch, and put some gas in the fuckin' car."

People began to stare.

Up walked Sherm, looking extracrispy in white linen.

"What'chu doing in the land, cuz? I thought you made a run down south."

"I been back, cuz. Just gettin' my shit worked on. Finding about them new grilles right there."

"Yeah, my transmission was fucked up, had to just go get my shit fixed up, too."

Twilight nodded at Sherm's watch. "I see you got the little Rolee on."

Sherm smiled. "Lil' sumpthin', a lil' fling, fling, know what I'm talkin' 'bout? Get my lil' shine on. I'm about to go get me some antifreeze over at Rothschild's. You ridin'?"

"Fa shizzle. Hol' on though. I'm still getting my gas."

"Oh, no—you got the bitch pumpin' gas."

Twilight shrugged. "This is real, live hundred percent pimpin', know what I'm talkin' 'bout? So she gotta be a hundred percent soldier. I can't deal with no less."

"You a col' dude," Sherm said, studying Remy. "I'm rolling with you then, lead the way."

Once Remy finished, Twilight shifted gears, and took off, on a night flight to see what they could get into. They stopped for a refill of "antifreeze," as Twilight liked to call alcohol.

"What we drinkin' tonight?" Sherm ask from out his car window.

"Crown, niggah. You know the routine."

Stacked with two bottles of Crown and some Henny for security, they headed toward the lake, racing down Lakeshore Drive at ninety and ninety-five miles an hour, weaving through light traffic. Suddenly the niggah Vogue rode up between them in a white Lexus on dubs. Twilight was in a champagne-colored Cadillac on Daytons, subwoofer pumping that first Comptons Most Wanted into the atmosphere. Sherm's Lincoln swerved to the middle lane and floored it past him. Twilight laughed and pulled deep off a blunt of some Hawaiian chronic, and sped up alongside him, the streetlights and the highway lines zooming by, turning into superimposed rhythms, the light dancing off the spiraling of his rims, fluctuating time and space, under the throaty purr of his machine.

When they got to Marty's, Charmaine's Silver Spur Rolls-Royce sat glistening in the parking lot. Irene and Remy got out and went to the locker room to change. When they walked in, Alizé was dancing on the small stage. The lights were dim and the DJ had just put on some up-tempo Jay-Z. The girls began to bounce when Twilight spotted Charmaine on the far side of the bar in heavy conversation with the manager, Patch.

Patch, an old friend of his mother's, stood up at the sight of Twilight. "C'm'ere, bwoi. I want you to meet this man. Twi, this is King Sugar Charmaine. Sugar, this is my god-son, Twilight."

"I know this young player already!" Charmaine gave Twilight a wink. "He showed me a thing or two out in Vegas. This here is an up-and-comer, Patch. A natural. How you this evening?"

"Slow motion, King Sugar, but ever dippin', never slippin'. Always elevatin' and pen-etratin'."

"That's right, baby. My motto is, 'If you can believe it and conceive it, then you can achieve it,' ya dig?"

" 'Ey, you my hero. I'm just tryna keep up with the Joneses and get my rightful share of the shine."

"Well, that ain't no terrible ambition to strive for, but all you see comes at a cost. Motherfuckers used to laugh at me. Call me clown. I been motherfuckin' 'buked and I been scorned, ya dig? Comin' up wasn't no day at the beach. But I'm still here, in the flesh. Looking better than ever."

"Got your stripes, huh?"

"Got my stars and stripes, jack. 'Cause I'm that motherfuckin' mack, selling cat an' collectin' traps. Dig what I'm sayin'?—I get that ho money. Now that ho money is slow money . . ."

"But it's sho money," Twilight finished.

"My man." They laughed and gripped fists. Charmaine passed the Moët around.

A trio of skinny, white Internet geeks, millionaires on paper as of that afternoon, watched Remy dance on the table. They slipped dollars in her slight bikini shorts as she raised one of her legs into a standing split. She began to flex her ass cheek to the rhythm,

and the three of them went crazy. She got down on all fours in front of the geekiest of the three and made her pussy pop, which sent him into a red-faced frenzy. He quickly finished his drinks and asked her "if it would be possible" to have a private dance in the back.

Not five minutes later, a phalanx of police stormed into the place. Marty's was being raided, and Patch quietly got up to speak with the Captain.

If you Love

me, I

# Devotion

What goes through a ho's mind?

The prostitute is at the center of the life—without her there *is* no life—and yet she is the most mysterious player in it. Why does she do it? What is it that motivates her, not only to rent out her body but to turn over the profits to another person, much less to someone who treats her like shit?

Maybe Remy could tell you. It was Valentine's Day, and just like every Valentine's Day, Garfield, Vogue, and Sherm hosted a Playerettes' Ball. This was the one night of the year the girls had off. They spent the day getting their hair done in tight marcels, curls, and beehives. There was a dress code for the night, and it was only one rule: everyone come attired in red, white, or both. Naturally, the decor was red and white, and there were

hearts, cupids, and silhouettes of the zodiac signs all over. In honor of the patron saint of lovers, the ladies colored their hair burgundy, sported rose tattoos, lacquered on candy-apple red lipstick, and broke out red fishnet stockings. Others wore white pearls, white satin teddies, white-lace thigh-highs and matching garter belts—they looked like brides on their wedding nights who left their husbands in the honeymoon suite and never looked back.

There was endless checking out of the competition, eyes on thighs, on the diamonds dangling between titties, dripping off bracelets, or magically glued to naked flesh. The players sported suits tailored for the occasion in different cuts and patterns but mostly in shades of red—scarlet, burgundy, crimson, mauve, wine—and wherever they stood together one saw a sea of red, choppy, surging, never still. There was a buffet and champagne reception, little meatballs on toothpicks, the usual buffalo wings, greens, mac 'n' cheese, and as a centerpiece a heart-shaped three-tiered cake with white icing, the third tier topped by a cupid in profile. To the left of the crowd, a stable of girls was gathered in a circle drawing the attention of the audience. In the middle was a thick, dark-skinned girl wearing a heart-shaped red bikini top and holding a long string of pearls in her hands. She made her ass clap to the beat in a pair of white short shorts.

Price limped in already tipsy, slurping Alizé out of an iced goblet, a woman on each arm. He caught Remy's eye. "Well, looky here, if it ain't Miss Susie Choosy herself. Remy, Remy, Remy, how is yuh? You still out here lawless in this cruel world?" He waved his cane majestically from his soapbox, his voice rising to the pitch of a country Baptist minister. "Still out here in this cruel world, lawless? Baby, yuh know what you need?" He handed her his business card. "You need some *God* in your life!" By now his eyes were gleaming with the zeal of a prophet.

She gave him a teasing look over her shoulder. "He's always been in my life. I don't know what you talkin' 'bout. I don't need nothing. I'm just fine."

"I've heard it before from you hos. Well, look, take my card 'cause yuh talkin' good but yuh lookin' rusty. You could have more, beautiful as you is. Believe me . . ." He got up close and personal, his eyes inches from hers, gold winking from his mouth. "*You could have more. Maybe we can have some private Bible study.*" He stroked his fur with his immaculately groomed and manicured fingers. "I can make you a real believer and achiever."

Behind him the awards ceremony was getting started. They were giving out the usual trophies in honor of Valentine's Day: Bitch of the Year, Tramp of the Year, and Ho of the Year. It was that way between pimps and their hos. Everything was a roast, a friendly humiliation.

"Bitch of the Year goes to Lisa. Lisa, where you, girl?" Nowhere to be seen was where, and to make matters worse, her uncle had to accept her award. "It's a true story," he slurred. "She's Bitch of the Year. It's a true story. But she couldn't be here today, on account of she got in a car accident. But I'm her uncle, and I will accept this honor in her place."

Remy rolled her eyes at Vogue, and they both laughed. She knew him from Atlanta. In truth, he had started her in this game, back when she was just dancing at the strip joints Magic City and Blue Flame. Sometimes she'd leave the club to dance with some of the other girls at an after session. Vogue came in one night and tipped her fifty dollars in ones and suggested that they talk once she got off. She stepped her pretty little ass off stage and went over.

He kept flashing his jewelry: watchband of brushed gold, thick gold links dangling from his ear lobes, gold chains around his neck (he wore five at time), and gold links in the shape of the letter "V" binding his French cuffs.

He grabbed her hand as if to kiss it, then flicked his tongue between her fingers. She pulled her hand away and wiped it for him to see.

Even stranger than Vogue were his women. They would be dressed up wearing no panties, flashing the tricks in the club. But if he walked over they froze on the spot—it was like his presence said, "Have your fun, but don't cross the line." No surprise that Remy got a strange feeling every time she saw him in the club.

His bottom was Ruby, a seasoned ho from Georgia. She used to be a dancer herself. She wore a silver-and-gold Rolex and matching gold tennis bracelets. She was a wonder of nature: she could clap her ass as loud as thunder. She had huge breasts and a butt with a twenty-two-inch waist dividing them, and a gold belly chain she wore to accentuate the feature. Ruby also carried two guns: one was a .45 she used as a warning and the other was a derringer, which she kept in a purple Crown Royal bag where she stuffed her bills, just in case someone was foolish enough to think the .45 was *just* a warning.

She always greeted Remy warmly when they saw each other in the locker room. "Hey, dahlin'. You all right this evenin'?" Remy thought her kind and sincere, real motherly, the type of woman she could really talk to. So one day when Ruby invited her for an early dinner, she accepted the invite and took a cab to the house, which Ruby paid for, telling her to keep the change.

The whole place, as much as Remy could see, was decorated in a color she could only describe as cream, but a cream that made you think the walls were made of cake frosting, with gold accents on everything. There was a cream-and-gold Steinway grand floating on a cream shag carpet, cream leather sofas and chairs, and in the middle with its back to the door a bone and leather throne with . . . her heart stopped. Vogue was sitting there in the living room, waiting.

Chills raced up her spine. "Oh shit," she thought. "He's trying to recruit me." She tried to stay calm.

Because Vogue wouldn't so much as speak to Remy unless she was dressed, Ruby brought her into a bedroom where five outfits lay across the round bed. Ruby told Remy

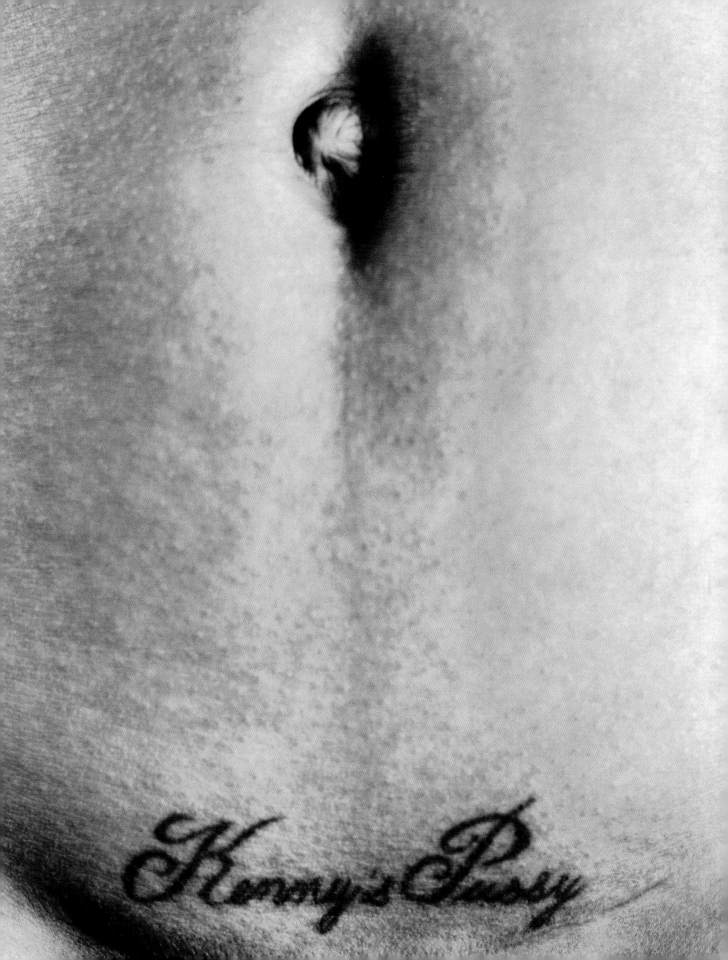

to get undressed and then come into the bathroom. In the pink-tiled room she washed Remy's face and then made her up again.

"You ever dated any of the guys in the club?"

"No."

"You afraid to make money?"

Remy fell silent. Her heart pounded. Ruby fixed a couple of Remy's stray curls, then brought her back to the bedroom where the outfits were laid out for her.

"Choose one."

Remy was shaking. She dressed slowly, her thoughts knotted up like a traffic jam. When she walked out into the living room, Vogue turned in his chair.

"I knew you would be with me."

On the way to dinner, Vogue explained things from the backseat.

"Look, you can either triple your money or stay a broke bitch. One or the other. The choice is yours." He sat in the back speaking into two cell phones in two different languages Remy didn't understand. She thought maybe one of them was Spanish, but she wasn't sure.

He ended both calls and leaned forward, touching his lips to her ear. "I have to work for *you* tonight. We gon' have dinner, have a lovely time. And then you gonna let me know if you down with us."

At the restaurant Remy played with her shrimp and salad, finally mustering the courage to tell him her intentions.

"I don't wanna be a ho. For you or nobody else."

"Well, I respectfully decline your offer," he said, with a wave of his hand. "You could have been making three times what you making now, and I don't like dealing with no idle, stupid ho."

And that was that. Remy felt like the choice had been taken away from her, and it was a relief not to have to make it herself. They stayed together for a few months, doing some sneak thieving and running the badger game on some convention tricks at the L.A. Hilton. One evening, Vogue came into the hotel room she was working out of and looked at the money on the table. He counted it twice.

"This it? Bitch, you holding out on me! Take your fucking clothes off! Come on, open up." He jammed his fingers up inside her. He knew she wasn't holding out on him—he just wanted to remind her who was in control. But that was enough. It was too much.

When they got back to Atlanta, she ran off.

She renegaded for a time, dancing in little after-hours sets once the clubs let out. Her girl would collect the money. "Where them dollars at? Ain't *nothin'* goin' down till I see some money!" Twenty men crowded her as she slowly opened her blouse to reveal her brown nipples, then she lay back on the carpet, raised her legs to reveal her shaved pussy, raised them over her head. The men gripped singles in their paws, faces frozen in anticipation as she closed her eyes and tried to escape to somewhere else.

That was when she met Twilight. They met at the Room under the circling lights. Twilight seemed to know all about her from the moment he said his first words. She had never heard the creed of pleasure articulated so eloquently. The language of the player makes anything sound appealing, but the logic behind it is simple: you're already doing it, so why not be organized about it? Get corporate about it.

He let her watch his flirty grin grow slowly. "Look at you, all fightin' against smilin'. What you got against smilin', baby?"

"I don't need a man calling me bitch and ho all day," she countered.

"Bitch and ho? It's more like baby and honey with me, darling. You ain't been dealing with the right type of man."

She gave him a lap dance, rubbing against him and pulling at his dick.

That night when they were going at it, she placed his hands on her throat, moaning under his hands, begging for annihilation. "Kill me, Daddy." She sucked in air against the pressure of his hands, pressure she was making with her own. "Choke me, Daddy. If you love me . . . kill me."

But he didn't love her.

He slowly loosened the grip she was trying to force him to make and started caressing her neck. "Nuh-uh. Ain't gonna be no killing. It ain't like that. I want you to live so you can get to mashing and stashing like you oughta be."

As Twilight's stable grew, so did his business sense, and slowly, so did his cruelty. The last two years he maintained a stable four to six women deep, and almost drama-free, as far as that was possible, and his hos weren't bringing in less than $15,000 a week. If the market dried up, he'd bring his steadiest girls to Atlanta or Vegas or Cancun. But then his girls started getting picked up regularly. When Irene, showing signs of jealousy, began to demand more attention, Twilight had her recruit for him, as punishment for making trouble. That evening she got picked up and was gone. It started with her, and it kept getting worse.

He thought about how other pimps handled their stables, each with a different management style. Amateurs gave their women free rein, but they didn't last. Vogue only *seemed* to let his women hang loose, but at the end of the night they hung off his neck like jewelry. Sugar was a firmer hand and had a tighter grip on his hos, so his family was tight-knit and well disciplined; he wasn't above beating his women in the shower or bringing his chrome piece to bed for the purpose of—as he put it—"putting the fear of Sugar in them"; but even so they had fun. Sometimes Sugar would get on the dance floor with all of his girls, tap his cane on the floor, and like some kind of voodoo priest, dance in a strange, mystical circle. His girls would gather around him and begin an unholy rocking, some breaking down to the floor to bow and touch his feet. It was something to see. Compared to Sugar, Twilight was morning dew on red rose petals—or maybe more like quiet anger wrapped in a mellow wine finesse.

But there had to be some golden mean, something practical between worship and chaos. There had to be, because Twilight felt like he was getting slack. He'd even let that one—what was her name?—Tisha, get away with smoking his money. He sincerely wanted to put a foot up her ass. She disappears for days, then one day shows up at his crib looking and talking crazy with some bullshit story and none of his money.

"Bitch, you must wanna die coming here." But Tisha, shit, Tisha was sixty-five girls ago, when he didn't even know how good he had it. Tisha gone, Remy gone, Irene gone . . .

# *Baptism*

In the early morning dark, Twilight found himself anointing his latest cuff in the dim lights of his back room. She was a young, fine-looking Russian he found dancing in some nowhere town in south Illinois. She told him her name was Maya, though he reminded himself not to believe a word she said. She was twenty-one with no family to speak of—Momma was a dust addict, and the older cousins she lived with used to touch on her every chance they got.

He didn't even remember how he'd convinced her to get in the Fleetwood, but he had, somehow. She was the darkest, countriest white girl he had ever laid eyes on, with enough ass, he figured, to reestablish himself in the game. Without Irene, things were looking bleak. The police had taken the Jaguar and it was getting harder and harder to

operate in the Chi. He hated to think about it, but it might be time to get rid of his two baby alligators pretty soon now, and it wasn't like he could just flush them down the toilet anymore. . . .

While they were driving up to Milwaukee, the setting sun turned the Wisconsin sky a peach color as Twilight looked on Maya, now fast asleep, and thought about how he almost didn't make the trip.

The pimp god, he laughed to himself, works in mysterious ways.

Maya looked like an earner, maybe more than Irene and Remy put together. And she had chosen. After three bleary days and nights of private riot, smashed Moët bottles, and midmorning laughter, she had chosen him. He ordered her then and there to "strip nekkid," and for the first time in three days, Maya hesitated at his instruction.

"You ain't gonna put them back in their tanks?" She said in her soft Russian accent, eyeing the two four-foot alligators named Knowledge and Understanding. The gators slowly roamed around the bedroom floor, staring and hissing.

"This their house," Twilight said. "You the visitor here. Now go on, take that shit off."

He had seen Maya naked already, but in the muted light of his bedroom, she was something truly remarkable. Her flawless skin and firm legs and thighs were the marks of a Thoroughbred. Twilight unbuttoned his shirt and reached under his bed for a large bottle of Jamaican overproof rum. He splashed it all over her naked flesh until her laughing turned to screams.

" 'Ey, what you screamin' in my house for?" Twilight whispered, dragging his words.

"My eyes," Maya whimpered, rubbing and blinking like a baby in the tub.

"Lay back. This a baptism. This is your anointing, ho. You need to be cleansed. We talkin' a new beginning for you. I'm a take away your pain—all that pain and shit in the past is gone now, baby. 'Cause from this motherfuckin' moment heah, you motherfuckin' Twilight's bitch, y'unnerstan'? You Twilight's property now." He rubbed the hot rum on her lips and neck. "You mine now. I want you to say it." He splashed more rum onto his fingers.

"I'm Twilight's bitch."

"And that means that tonight you go out and strap on your ho boots an' ho up, y'unnerstan', work that magic. Dis some real pimpin' here, and if you tryna be a part o' *me* you gotta play *your* motherfuckin' part." The rum made slow progress down her stomach, pooling at her deep belly button and lingering in the light brown hair that trailed from it. He burned the rest of the white rum down his throat, lifting her off the bed and up against the wall. "But that's after. After we celebrate you being with a real pimp, live in the flesh."

Knowledge, his cragged jaws agape, stared at them in ancient, unblinking stillness.

But Maya's past was not rubbed and caressed away so easily. Twilight was not her first pimp and would not be her last. She was mixed up, and there was a cunning to her confusion. She was from Russia, yeah, but via Detroit, where she had had a high-paying trick that she had wrapped around her oversized clitoris. She would meet him at the Temple Hotel, and he would stare but she would not let him touch it until he bowed down to her pussy and paid cash tribute to it. Then and only then would she let him worship her with his tongue.

She had way too much extended family in Detroit so she hit the road freelance, only to find that worshipers didn't come so easy as that first one. She needed management, and she met Twilight when she still held possibilities in her body, before all the angels had abandoned her. He talked to her like she was a woman. Like she meant something. He was draped in all the signs of getting paid, the shiny trinkets of false salvation. And she bought it, hook, line, and sinker, even as she knew it was a lie. She gave in to all the potential disasters crowding around her, knew it when she did it, and that hot summer she became the queen of hell right alongside her demonic prince Twilight, who helped chase the rest of her angels away.

♦   ♠   ♥   ♣

That afternoon Twilight fell into a heavy slumber. He dreamed he was walking through the sprawling backwoods of his childhood, back in Jackson, down through those muddy paths dressed in his Easter best—pink velour suit turning into white Gucci fur turning into . . . whatever it was, they were the wrong clothes to be wearing out in these damp woodlands. He tried in vain to tread lightly over the thick soup impeding his progress, all the while his fur, his pants, everything, got splattered, soiled, and made unworthy—ruined. He kept walking anyway, down toward the sound of a river. And standing there under the gray sky and dark crisscross of trees was old man Aarons, the original pimp-daddy Mr. Elijah himself, speechifying.

"The truth is I was never truly myself," Elijah said, talking without moving his lips. "I was never the master of my own action, only captive of my circumstances. This sort of man becomes an echo of someone else's music. It is with the luxury of regret that I tell you these things."

Twilight suddenly found himself seized by thirst. He splashed waist-deep into the river only to realize it wasn't gushing water but blood that smelled of rum. Twilight looked down into it and saw the shapes of dead bodies under the water. On the surface he caught a glimpse of his face, distorted in the thick, moving liquid. It was a reflection of someone he no longer knew. Something about it felt erotic, and suddenly some quiet, creeping horror came over him like a sickness and he awoke to find Maya deep-throating him.

A day later she was gone—disappeared. That's all right, he told himself, they don't come to stay, they come to play, and they come to pay; but he didn't buy it.

It baffled Twilight, this quivering in him that wouldn't let up. *What part of the game was this?* he wondered.

He went driving in the Monte Carlo that evening, riding on the asphalt skin of Milwaukee. The ride was a nice piece of street jewelry, turning colors in the sun, a chariot rolling on twenties that announced his arrival in the manner of Gabriel's trumpets. His instructions to the rims guy was it had to be fly enough to make a hater cry, *"Ai-right!"*

Steady now . . .

He had been through all kinds of shit in this game. He'd seen triumphs turned tragedy and vice versa. He flashed back to his hungriest year as a child on the West Side of Chicago, back when his father had already disappeared into forever. He thought about the time he cried when he heard Curtis Mayfield sing, "We can deal in rockets and dreams, but reality—what does it mean?" He felt his own guts starting to rebel against him.

He threw up out the side window. First it was clear, like oil, no content, but the second heave gave blood. Now he was scared.

The dream was unnerving him.

# Slippin' into Darkness

The last Players' Ball of the millennium was a week later. It was a night that stood out from the thousands of late nights in the long night of his life. He pulled up to it in the Monte Carlo swerving into the lake-sized parking lot of the Club. The boulevard outside the lot was an opulent driveway, bumper-to-bumper slick cars, pretty vessels old and new: Bentleys, Benzes and El Dorados, Excaliburs and Jaguars, Lamborghinis and Lincoln stretch Town Cars. It looked like the setting of a Hollywood premiere, with the red carpet, the Kliegl lights cutting swaths in the sky, and hired photographers popping a half dozen flashes for every car that rolled up.

The Club was one of those classic midsixties catering halls, a one-floor castle made from the finest stucco and fiberglass mob money can buy, hosting a dozen or so party rooms with identical decor. Each one had red imitation-leather banquettes, tables nailed

to the floor to prevent possible brawls, wall-sized mirrors veined with gold paint, and red lamps hanging with faux Venetian glass. In the Empire Room, the size of a half-height airplane hangar, multicolored paper streamers draped from the four corners of the mirrored ceiling to the center of the room, where the mirrored disco ball hung, raining shards of light like confetti over the walls and the arriving crowd.

They were dressed to kill, players from all area codes in top-price shit, embroidered silk suits in primary colors, big shoulders, wide lapels, and matching gators, Mauris in gold, two-toned spectators everywhere. The room was full of ballers whose gear said "money" but didn't bother to whisper it. The mirrored ball cast gold and silver over elaborate beehives, waterfalls, and other sculpted hairdos, every head in the room either done up or wide-brimmed and topped with a three-inch crown. Every finger was weighed down with ice, gold or platinum. Every single article people wore was a proud tribute to conspicuous consumption.

The DJ was playing dusties. He threw on the Whispers, "Lost and Turned Out," and everybody was stepping Chicago style as a suited and booted crowd arrived.

Twilight's few remaining girls were locked up, so he walked in and took his spot among the congregation of ghetto princes crowding under the mirrored ceiling and wine-red lights of the Club. The place was full of hands raised in the air in mock praise. There were umm-hmms and explosions of style: even a baby pimp in a cream-pink jumpsuit, pristine finger waves increasing in height and weight in fluid increments, from hairline to the middle of his back.

Twilight kept the smile where it needed to be, but he still didn't feel right. He couldn't shake it. And it didn't help that the place had no real ventilation. He felt lightheaded moving through all the assorted flavors of smoke, from pungent stogies to sweet, aromatic tobacco and blunts. The feeling got even stronger, but he fought the discomfort by adding a roll to his gait and a deceptive gaze for all those watching.

"My man, Twilight!" Vogue greeted him with a pound.

"Twilight!" said someone else, slapping hands with him.

Twilight traded jokes with Lance and Mojo, still somehow coming up with all the right witticisms and pleasantries. He made sure he stayed sharp all night: teardrop diamond ring, mahogany cane, snakeskin belt, and a platinum chalice with his name etched in its side filled with Crystal and ice—all the trimmings.

But sharp as he looked, he was just one of many glittery and immaculate men of odd circumstance in all their finery, wearing python skins, Borsalino hats, and brightly colored suits of every flavor with matching pocket squares, while stepping out of either a white Lexus on bravas or a candied Cadillac sitting on dubs or out of a ragtop Benze. They entered trailed by stables, laying their cellies down at the bar as they made it known how good the game had been to them. While they signed and signified, the players and macks, exchanging laughter and tossing it up, new Jezebels and seasoned felines could be seen from all over.

War's "Slippin' into Darkness" blasted from the floor speakers when Big Sharky arrived dressed head-to-toe blue-and-black python with a line of new girls in his stable, all wearing different styles of dresses that matched his suit. They followed him in a serpentine line, each with her forehead placed in the small of another's back, the centipede changing directions with his slightest move until he finally dismissed them for the moment.

The international players made their appearances: Lance, P-waukee's own Father Heavenly, and Danny Oakley in their floor-length minks with matching crowns; Virgo, the pimp magnificent and his family, who came with the express purpose of having fun; and dozens of others smoking and leaning in their pedicures and Mauri sandals. Garfield passed out mimeographed copies of the ballot for Player of the Year:

# Twenty-First-Century Players

## THE MARVELOUS GENTLEMEN PLAYERS' BALL BALLOT SLIP

### RULES:

You May Not Vote for Yourself!!!

Check One Contestant Only or Ballot Will Be Void.

Only Pimps Can Vote

All Ballots Must Be Turned In by 1:00 A.M.

There Will Be a Runner-up for Pimp of the Year

## CANDIDATES

☐ Pimp Vogue        ☐ Kool-Aid                  ☐ Coal Black

☐ Price             ☐ Money                     ☐ Le Kid

☐ Pimp Chi          ☐ Milk                      ☐ Mellow Drama

☐ The McNeals       ☐ Sir Rick                  ☐ Lord Henry

☐ Pimp Red          ☐ Billion                   ☐ Pillow Talk

☐ Ju-Ju             ☐ White Folks               ☐ Mojo

☐ Good-Game         ☐ The Dream Merchants       ☐ Pimp Nine

☐ Pimpin' Ken       ☐ Virgo                     ☐ Quickfast

☐ Pimp Shy          ☐ Sir Lancelot              ☐ Teardrop

☐ Pimp Twilight     ☐ Pimp J.C.                 ☐ Pimp Divine

                    ☐ Playboy

In Case There Is a Tie, There Will Be a Runoff for the Tiebreaker

Near the bar, two hos, Misha—one of Vogue's girls—and LeAnn, a renegade from St. Louis, got to screaming at each other, then started grabbing at hair and clothes. When security finally broke them up, LeAnn found herself thrown out into the parking lot wearing nothing but five-inch pumps and a red thong, her bare nipples hardening in the cold air. Two bouncers watched her stagger away mumbling to herself, like this was the sort of thing that happened to her all the time.

But it wasn't, and the uproar started a chain of events. Distracted by the fight, someone at the bar knocked over a tray of drinks, all of them crashing to the floor. Miss Maxine, proprietor of the Club, started screaming for people to back up with such vigor that her teeth went airborne and fell onto the bar. Everyone's eyes bulged in disbelief. She quickly grabbed her teeth and stuffed them back into her mouth. Silence, then an explosion of muffled laughter and teary eyes.

Nothing else happened for a time, but something in the air made it feel like anything could happen at that moment.

In the meantime, ladies slow-dragged their asses across the dance floor like they were towing heavy weight. They danced back and forth, waiting for the moment that the speakers would really start playing the deeper bass that ultimately moved them.

"The Chairman of the Board has arrived!"

That meant the evening now had its master of ceremonies. It was Price, and he started making pronouncements the moment he walked through the door. He came in with his bottom, Mimi, who had gotten him through the most difficult times. She had, as Price said time and again, made the sacrifice. And so now she was honored as his primary.

Price mounted the stage, and after greeting the other luminaries from across the country, he took the mike.

"Yuh *know* . . ." He let his words hang in the air as everybody turned toward him;

he milked the pause, and people laughed like he was tickling them. "Yuh know . . . not everybody can do this!" Price's voice boomed, the thud of his iced fingers resonating from the mike through the hall, and the crowd boomed back at him: *YAY-uh! You know that's right! That's what* I'm *sayin! Not everybody can do dis shit!*

He hollered at the top of his lungs, "*Play* that playah music!" Looking around, he shouted, "What we workin' with tonight? Let's see . . . what we workin' with? Bring 'em up, y'all!"

As hands rose in the air at the first notes of "I Choose You," the intro looped seamlessly a dozen or so times to build momentum. Price introduced players, greeted guests, acknowledged family, friends, constituents, industry people. "First of all, I'd like to thank all the undercovers for coming out and supporting us tonight." The crowd gave a big, sarcastic cheer, looking around laughing, here and there a *Hear, hear!*

When the song hit its climax, "Then no longer do I have to shop around anymore," Price bellowed, "This is Hollyhood! Hollyhood, y'all! Hollyhood, y'all! Yes suh! Talk like a playah!" Strobes flashed from the background, where player after player posed for family portraits. Everyone knew the words—some even bowed their heads like it was the secret national anthem, a sacred song. Others stared smiling at Price as he worked the crowd, wearing a sharp white Borsalino with gray trim, his hair buttered and in a mini-ponytail, laughing at the eager MC wannabes trying to grab the mike and represent.

"Is this what we workin' with?" he said, coming down off the stage with all the smooth confidence of Superfly hosting a beauty pageant. "Yuh know, not everybody . . ." he paused again, and this time the crowd chorused back, *Can do this!*

Price nodded with approval.

"Yuh know what I'm saying?" Another chorus back, this time *Mmm-hmm* and

*Oh, yeah!* "Aw, no—not everybody can do this . . ." The crowd was laughing with him again. ". . . *church!*" The crowd whooped with him: *Chuch! Chuch!*

He took off his hat, whipped out a crimson silk pocket square, and wiped the sweat from his brow beneath the buttered bangs plastered against his forehead. "Y'all be cool, and listen to the minister . . . y'all listen to the good Reverend Price." *Preach it, bruthah!* "I'm preachin' it! Oh yeah, I'm preachin' it! Now yuh know I'm in the church I just come to show my love for, and I—"

Before he could finish the crowd started laughing and applauding. He soaked it up for a minute, then acknowledged a player just entering the room. "How you doin', bruthah? We thought you weren't gonna show up, muh bruthah, on this beautiful day. I see you up in here, Kool-Aid, glad you could make it. Give it up for the macks and playahs, y'all!" Thunderous waves of applause. "These boys come from all ovah. . . . All ovah . . . all the way from HuhWAH-ee . . . Noo Yawk . . . Washington Dee-Cee. . . . And yuh know they representin' . . . to represent. . . . Yuh know we gonna make this biggah than it's evah been. We gonna start this here new millennium off with a BANG, y'all! And every year it's gonna grow and grow. . . . We standin' on that!"

The crowd was whooping and hollering, *Chuch! Chuch! Hear, hear! You know that's right!*

"There's some *pimps,* some *hustlahs,* some *playahs* up in this plizzaad!—got-DAMN!" his voice booming, his feet stomping. "We gon' have *church* up in heah!" And the people responded with shouts of *Chuch!* and *Tell it!*

The crowd was getting warm, but it wasn't yet hot, not as hot as it needed to be. Everyone was still too self-conscious to have a good time. The pimps who had come with their entire stables were like team captains—both the leader and the star. When Vogue went to the bathroom to primp and preen and return, his girls would make sure that he

was all right before he reentered the room. And all the rest of the pimps took their turns doing the same thing.

"I'm a run down the program for all y'all, give y'all a taste of what's to come. First, we got the presentation of our out-of-town guests and celebrities. Then we got the Erotic Battle Royale of the Millennium between Ms. Diva and Ms. Infinitee. *Yeah!* Next up after that we got the Players' Ball Best-Dressed Contest, judged by Signore Domino and Salon Chicago—gonna be a tight contest, tell you what!" Big noise from the crowd. "But wait now, wait now—then we got the prestigious presentation of the Lifetime Achievement Award, followed by the fabulous Players' Ball Raffle with all kinds of prizes. And then . . . and then . . . and then—yeah, you *know* what's next!—the *climax* of the evening, the awards presentation and Grand Finale of the ball, the nineteen hundred and ninety-nine Player and Pimp of the Year Contest!"

The crowd went wild, whooping, shrieking, howling—that's what it was all about.

Price tapped the mike. "Now I have a question. I have a question, and a burning need for an answer. I need an answer, and I need to know, and I need to know *now*"— the crowd was starting to get worked up, he was playing them like a first-class preacher— "*Who's that real pimp?*"

With that, the pimp stroll contest began, and with it, the evening began for real. First Vogue came across the stage dipping and twirling.

"*Who's that real pimp?!*"

Next Mojo in a white fur with a red collar and matching gators took a statesman-like turn.

"*Who's that real pimp?!*"

The audience answered him: *Pimp! Pimp! Pimp!*

Billion strolled in wearing an ice-cream seersucker suit, spats, and a straw boater,

then Pimp Chi came out in a tangerine three-piece with matching crocheted hat and cape, looking like he'd just jumped out of the seventies.

*"Who's that real pimp?"*

*Pimp! Pimp! Pimp!*

Virgo came in, tresses cascading over his fur, with an army of hos, ten in all, wearing matching red lace.

"Who's that real pimp?" Price kept asking.

*Pimp! Pimp! Pimp!* the crowd returned.

*Pimp! Pimp! Pimp!*

Twilight was a rising star for long enough that he now had to be considered "established." At least if no one knew the curveballs he'd been thrown in the last few weeks, and no one there could know. Around one thirty, Price started reading the announcements, and Twilight was suffering. A feeling strong enough to make him sick.

The presentation of the awards was gearing up. Price's voice was a little raspy, but still rolling. He was saying something about somebody, and Twilight suddenly realized that Tango was at the side of the stage, and he was the somebody Price was talking about. ". . . so let's give this old player a chance to say something. He's got this lifetime achievement locked down—wasn't even a contest about it. And the things he says . . . yeah, the things he says, they can teach us *all* a lesson. Not just you up-and-comers, but those of us who think we're old-timers—I say who *think* we're old-timers!" Warm laughter from the crowd. "That's right. 'Cuz this player was there from the git-go and still going strong. So now, without any further ado, ladies and gentlemen, I give you the winner of the Millennium Lifetime Achievement Award, the man himself, the master, the maharaja, the grand pooh-bah of pussy, ladies and gentlemen, I give you . . . *Pimp Tango!*"

Tango ambled up onto the stage, tricked out in a suit made of butter-soft calf leather, and bowed at the waist to accept his award from Price. He stood facing the crowd as the

applause washed over him, his weathered face breaking up in a smile. "Thank you. Thank you. This is a great night. A great night for me, a great night for the game. I'd like to offer up this little toast as my way of saying thank you." He cleared his throat and started to recite from memory.

*My ride is a blue Caddy parked at the curb*
*A harem of fine hos do the deed by my word.*
*I'm known from New York to the Frisco Bay*
*For makin' bitches bow down and makin' tricks pay.*

*I'll put your girl in a trance,*
*Make her do the ho dance—*
*Just one* look *at the ho,*
*She drops drawers to the floor.*
*I'll be deep 'tween those thighs*
*While you rolling snake eyes.*
*Doctors look to analyze,*
*Give the grave diagnosis:*
*"It's that pimp niggah Tango,*
*hit your bitch with Pimpnosis."*

*Stay ass-getter, born mack-man supreme,*
*I don't just keep 'em mesmerized;*
*Fieree backbone-splitter, a rich whore's cream,*
*Hell, I don't even keep 'em* hyp*notized;*

*Smooth pussy-wetter, a poor bitch's dream*
*When a broad falls for me, she's* pimp*notized!*

*"So please, Dr. Tango—what's the prognosis?"*
*Just hit 'em off with a dose of Pimpnosis.*

*You got insufficient funds?*
*In my religion it's a sin*
*For a bitch to be down with no cash coming in.*
*Ho* needs *a good pimp if she's in it to win,*
*So let her come unto me if she's lacking direction—*
*I endow her with the power of the midsection.*

*No need to have a coronary thrombosis—*
*Dr. Tango is here, prescribing Pimpnosis . . .*

He went on, and the crowd lapped it up, yelling themselves hoarse when he finished. Twilight had the impulse to rush up and embrace the man, but shook his head and hung back while Tango soaked up the attention. He went back to his drink, or his drinks, or his drink after drink after drink.

He heard Price announce the Player of the Year. He heard his own name. Then he felt himself being pushed toward the stage.

Twilight picked up the statue in a haze and grabbed the mike. "I'm a always keep it P-I, international pimpin' worl'wide." Then he was back into the shadows and started chatting up a fine young filly in the corner as the crowd got hyped to hear the final

announcement of the night—Pimp of the Year. But Twilight wasn't listening anymore. Something wasn't right, and others sensed it. Eyes had followed him off the stage and people started talking. No one could remember seeing Twilight even the slightest bit off balance—and even a little meant way too much.

Twilight moved away from the crowd as he heard Mr. Elijah's voice echo in his mind. "I was never the master of my own action, only captive of my circumstances . . . an echo of someone else's music."

He reviewed the evening in his head again; the crowd, the applause, how everyone was hyped up throwing out their hands for pounds, the look in their eyes. But in the midst of the elevation he couldn't help but think on his girls knocked by the cops a week before the ball, and Charmaine, gone. It cut through the sweetness of the moment.

He had a sick feeling that shit was getting deep. He could keep a surface smile for the crowd and play it hard as concrete, but it only masked his inner turmoil and disgust.

*Playah of the Year,* he thought, *yeah . . . elevation. Elevation like a muthafuckah. Movin' up. But what does it mean without Sugar here, without King Sugar Charmaine?*

When he had picked up his trophy he'd heard somebody who sounded like Price shouting, "I know you were going for Pimp of the Year—next time, next year," and as he made his way through the waves of approval, the sweet-and-sour smell of Newports and rum brought back the dream he'd had earlier.

He could feel the sweat rolling down his back, the pit of his stomach rumbling. He wondered if his smile looked as painted on as it felt. He knew he was immaculate. Everywhere he looked in the room he saw the mirror image of himself from all angles, while all the hustlers up in the Club hooted and hollered under the lights. He made his way through the crowd, stopping here or there to accept accolades from fellow players.

Just as he hit the door of the Club, past the velvet rope, a young player ran up to him, shouting, "Twilight! Twilight! You forgot your trophy!"

He had forgotten the winged lady. He eyed the prize, "International Player of the Year" was inscribed on the marble base. "Hey, thanks, young blood," he said, grabbing the award and crossing the street to the jammed and gleaming parking lot.

He turned the key in the ignition and set off to the other side of town, glancing at the gold-plated plastic trophy lying on the seat next to him. Then he looked in the rearview mirror and gazed at his own face. *The outside of a man,* he thought, *can never tell you about who he really is.* Surely there was no difference between him and Sugar's corpse, laid out in his finest, ready to serve as a sacrifice to the earth. He pictured them lowering Charmaine's casket into the ground and woke out of his daze just in time to find the Monte Carlo drifting off the Eisenhower. He quickly got hold of the wheel.

He'd have to go back—he'd missed the turn at the Dan Ryan.

Twilight regained his composure but couldn't erase the voices getting louder and louder in his head. It got even worse when they mingled with the sound coming out of his tape deck. The music was like church and a bar piano at the same time. The vocalist was singing about the rivers of his homeland, about searching. Twilight let his head be baptized by the cool water of the bruthah's tearful voice, and since he knew the words, he sang along.

" . . . I've got to change my way of living . . . !"

Nodding his head to the words, he suddenly realized he had to get out of the game.

He opened the window, hoping the predawn chill would wake him a little. The air was crisp, but still warm. The road was empty. His mind wandered to Jackson, to his head resting between his momma's bosom when he was a boy. Her smell of baby powder and tobacco and her telling him the only bedtime story he guessed she knew, the story of

Rasputin and Missy and how they created a prince. He tried to connect the image of the motherly poised woman who fawned over him, and whupped him when he got out of line, with the girl stumbling out of the passenger's seat of some man's rig at a truck stop in his youth.

He remembered one of Tango's teachings from the hole and whispered it to himself: *Through the invisible I sent my soul a letter from the afterlife, and by and by my soul returned to me and answered I myself am Heaven and Hell* . . .

He thought of Sherm, how from the time he was young Sherm wanted to pimp, how he was born with only the dream and none of the tools; how his cousin took second place all the time and allowed himself to be played by Twilight, even though he was older; how committed Sherm could be and how desperate he'd become. He'd broken Twilight's commandment, for as long as he'd been a player Twilight never had to raise his hand to take life. Sherm took life, and though Twilight felt justified in punishing him, he knew now that he lashed out at him because he *knew* Sherm would take it.

That's just who he was.

Then there was Angela. For the first time he thought about how they'd just grown apart. His hunger for the game left her in the distance. He took all he could from her and just kept on; she gave so easily. Sad, aging Angela gave him everything, even his name, and he let her go like a kid with a balloon, distracted as he was by all the other prizes of the game. There was a point where everything in his life accelerated and the more he tried to look back and make sense of it all, the more it became a blur of faces, leaving only one person anchored in all the chaos, and that was Charmaine. His mentor.

The closest thing he ever had to a father.

Twilight had a sudden realization then—a vision of a mountain of things, every beautiful ride he'd ever possessed, every piece of jewelry, all of it in a dirty heap and on top of it Charmaine; no, not Charmaine—Charmaine's corpse. Twilight shook his head at the vision. *Man,* he thought, *there's nothing left. Nothing.* But that wasn't right. He knew there had to be something of real value that King Sugar Charmaine had bestowed upon him. And then he remembered something Charmaine used to say all the time, something he never took to heart because he was so sure it didn't apply to him. "Quit while you're still on top, player. Y'hear me? Quit while you're still on top."

Maybe there were other games to play, other roads to take. His next thought was an image of himself still in the life, only someplace else—maybe Memphis, maybe Jackson—and the picture made him scowl. He was so deep in contemplating his next step that he never noticed the cop car till he saw red in the rearview mirror—red light, flashing bright, headed his way, tailing him, and the morning traffic was too tight to make a dash for it. He was trapped.

*Play it cool,* he thought, sweating in his suit. He realized he had been holding his breath, but he didn't know for how long—ten seconds? A minute? Five?

The light brightened as the police car drove up behind the Monte Carlo, pulled into the next lane, and then sped past him. Twilight breathed a sigh of relief and shook his head hard, like he was trying to wake himself from a bad dream.

*Damn,* he thought.

Signaling, he made a right into the next lane, eased back into his seat, and let the open road take him where he needed to go.

# *Final Toast*

May I Propose a Toast to My People . . . Trust is the currency and these are the people who are valuable to me. For as long as we stay oblivious to the other side's reality, we will be held responsible for their manipulation. For as long as we allow ourselves the luxury of passing our pain onto others, we remain in bondage. For as long as we seek the upper hand, the others' manners and reality will continue to define us all as a people. . . .

Whom do you belong to?

To my cousin Bruce Gage, for his support on this project.

A toast to King Bert, for his trust and understanding.

To King JoJo, for an open mind and his point of view.

Thank you, Franklin Sirmons, for knowledge and direction.

A special thank-you to Hyder Ali, my favorite landlord,

for having my back for three to six months.

A toast to Julian Schnabel, for introducing me

to Ingrid Sischy at *Interview* and for his priceless input.

Ingrid, for your interest and understanding.

Thank you *Life* magazine, for the nomination and

publishing my work, and your overall support.

Jack Woody of Twin Palms, for insight, information, and interest.

Manie Barron, my first editor, for grasping the whole concept

and the nature of the game.

Ralph Samuelson, a toast to you. Thank you for your support.

ACC/Rockefeller, for your support in the future.

Sarah Bradley and Margaret Cogswell A.C.C.

To Chozo and Hiromi Yoshi of Yoshi Galleries in Japan,

for years of support and for believing in my work.

Eli Kabillo, Mad Dog Films, for your support in the past, present, and future.

A toast to Terry Coleman.

To Auntie Felicia, who is always a source of inspiration and

for putting her two cents in.

A toast to Uncle Claude for his style and wit and for being a source of inspiration.

Honey Stewart, the source of all, the crib.

A toast to Kendall Lloyd.

To all my people in 662, 312, 773, and 702.

A toast to Rob Marriott.

Thank you, Alexandra Rowley, for your guidance and direction.

Susan Kismaric at MoMA, I send you all my blessing.

Bryan Adams at Soho Black and White NYC.

Monsieur Camp, Dupon, Paris.

David at I2I.

Laurent le Moing, for his magic touch.

Bob Kapoor and Chia at Duggals.

To the following people I would like to express *particular* appreciation:

My literary agent, Tanya McKinnon, of Mary Evans, Inc. I am eternally grateful.

Marielle Lifshitz and Tina D. Kourasis of Gardner Carton & Douglas

for having my back 100%.

My editor, Josh Behar, for his dedication to the project and making this happen.

Jo Obarowski, for great design and art direction.

And HarperCollins.

Bert, Big Lex, Bishop, Bo Mike, Capri, Casanova, Drop, Father Divine, Ford,

Good Game, Ice T, JoJo, Ju Ju, Kenny Ivey, King James, Kool-Aid, Mack Strong,

Miss May Masters, Miss Vogue, Money, Play Sister, Rook, Scorpio, Seymour,

Shooting Star, Shorty, Skooter G, Snub Nose, Tracey, Velvet, Vick

## A toast to . . .

Brian Adams, Chris Black, Knia Bond, Calbee Booth, Erik Buck, Carry Bullard, Michael Butler, George E. Cano-Moreno, Ruben Castillo, Bhaskar Chaliha, Shavanen Childs, Harry Davis, Daze, Delmar, the Diaz family, Latasha Natasha Diggs, Mr. Feliciano, Jena Ferguson, Fudge, Juan Gonzalez, Neil Grady, Dale Grant, Ramon Hall, Tony Hawk, Sam Hyde, Monte Isom, Yasuko Ito, Jones, Eli Kabillo, Kid Capri, Jerome Lagarrigne, Nemo Librizzi, Richard Maitland, Edwina Martin, Sandra Martinez, Terri McCoy, Jon Nakkano, Gregg O, Rodrick Perry, Phase 2, Happy Pontanares, Vanessa Rivera, Leon E. Robinson, Ernesto Rodriguez, Daniela Roebuck, Mario Sanabria, Dennis Sanchez, Silk, Richard Simon, Kevin Stabb, Lorna Thomas, the Torres family, Moselle Trim, Carolyn Williams, Richard Zuluaga

## Levons nos verres pour les miens

Stephanie Binet, Emmanuel de Burettec, Roxann Camp, Beatrice Cheramy, Masa Eguchi, Antoine Garnier, Françoise Leandre, Anne Lifshitz, Christophe Montout, Jon One, Ollyve Thalien, Toxic, Mark Zisman

## Kanpai

Chie, ECD, Fumiya Brown, Hashimoto family, Hashimoto Megumi, Hibi Kozo, Hibi Nanase, Hirata Norio, Hirata Sumio, Hosoe Eikoh, Ishii Akira, Ishii Rieko, Ishizaki Yuko, Kami, Kaneko Mami, Kuwahara Moichi, Maruno Asako, Master Key, Matsumoto family, Matsumoto Ruki, Mighty Crown, Mori Yukinojo, Nagai Seiji, Nagaoka Midori, Nyoro, Orang, Sakai Yoyo, Sakino Masaaki family, Sakurai Makiko, Sui-Ken, Sin, Takagi Kan, Takei Akiko, Ushiku Tatsumi, Watabe Ryu, Woodman, Yoshida Ruiko, Zeebra

—*Tracy Funches*

**God, Olodumare**

Eternal love and gratitude goes to Tanya McKinnon.

Thanks to Mary Evans and Josh Behar.

Many more thanks to the fam: Tracy Funches,

Sibi Lawson for her love and encouragement,

undiscovered Bronx genius Reginald Dennis Jr., comrade James Bernard,

twin brother Cheo Coker, Papa Peter Noel, Rob Kenner,

Jeaninne Amber for her patience and sacrifice, Carter Harris, Shani Saxon,

*Vibe* magazine, Herbie Raynaud, Sagal Abshir, Monica Williams,

Frances Bailey, Donna Bailey, Patricia Peters, My only sister Kimica, Richard Carey,

Chris Brown, Khem, Niko, Karl, Lorna, and Karif Marriott, Donald Ruff and family,

Mark White, Nnenna Onyuwuchi, Greg Tate, Vicki Campbell, Arthur Jafa.

Special thanks also to those who pulled my coat:

Bruce Gage and the entire staff of Mario Uomo, Sir George, Michael Ace,

Mr. White Folks, Money, Pimpin' Kenny Ivey, Sean Combs, Zaza, Outkast,

Fifty Grand, Voodoo, GOOD-GAME, Ju Ju, Kool Aid.

Keep it gangsta: Choise-One, Rome, Dave, J-Dot, Brucie B, Ed,

Obed and the entire 162 and Ogden, Ghost, G-Bone, and The 9-7 out in L.A.

Rest in Peace: Julio

—*Rob Marriott*

# Photographs

## FUNCHES STUDIO

O. Funches, executive director

Yasuko Ito, public relations director

Rick Perry, creative director

Maria Velasquez, staff

# In God We Trust

| | |
|---|---|
| Howard Funches | 1945–2002 |
| Anthony Al Clark | 1964–2001 |
| Lady Stardust | 1980–2001 |
| Victor de la Cruz | 1979–2001 |
| "Juleo" | 1978–2001 |
| Staga McKinley | 1969–2001 |
| Miss Concord | 1933–2001 |
| Thomas "Geepers" Jefferson | 1914–2001 |
| Jett | 1974–2000 |
| Channing Nigel Jacques | 1969–2000 |
| Alfred "Bilbo" Gholson | 1920–2000 |
| Quentin Crisp | 1910–2000 |
| Cornell Worthen | 1931–1999 |

# A Note About the Prints

All of the photographs reproduced in this book are gelatin silver prints. The prints are made on 11 × 14-inch paper and range in image size.

The printing date of the photographs ranges from the year of the negative to 2001. All of the prints are from the private collection of the Funches archives. Available at www.pimpnosis.com.